LOOK what I've MADE too!

● ● ● ● ● ● ●

Lots of great ideas for things to make, bake, paint and play

Melanie Rice
● ● ● ● ● ● ● ● ● ●

HODDER AND STOUGHTON
LONDON SYDNEY AUCKLAND

To Chris, Catherine and Alex, for all their help.

British Library Cataloguing in Publication Data

A catalogue record for this title is available from the British Library

ISBN 0 340 60409 3

Text copyright © Melanie Rice 1989, 1991
Illustrations copyright © Lynne Farmer 1989, 1991

This compilation first published 1993
Includes material used in Crafty Ideas series
(Hodder and Stoughton Children's Books 1989-91)

All rights reserved. No part of this publication may be reproduced or transmitted in any form or by any means, electronically or mechanically, including photocopying, recording, or any information storage and retrieval system, without either prior permission in writing from the publisher or a licence permitting restricted copying. In the United Kingdom such licences are issued by the Copyright Licensing Agency, 90 Tottenham Court Road, London W1P 9HE.

The rights of Melanie Rice to be identified as the author of the text of this work and of Lynne Farmer to be identified as the illustrator of this work have been asserted by them in accordance with the Copyright, Designs and Patents Act 1988.

Published by Hodder and Stoughton Children's Books, a division of Hodder and Stoughton Ltd, Mill Road, Dunton Green, Sevenoaks, Kent TN13 2YA

Design by Sally Boothroyd
Photographs by Chris Fairclough

Printed in Hong Kong by Colorcraft Ltd

CONTENTS

	Page
Photograph Tree	4
Repeating Patterns	6
Jewellery	8
Bottled Herbs	10
Miniature Garden	12
Bird Nest Potatoes	14
Eastern Delights	16
Chinese Dragon Salad	18
Greetings Cards	20
Desk Tidy	22
Fabric Painting	24
Tie and Dye Scarf	26
Moving Pictures	28
Window Picture	30
Acrobat	32
Chinese Dragon	34
Acrobatic Angler	36
Diving Octopus	38
Helicopter	40
Dart and Launcher	42
Gift Boxes	44
Fish Mobile	46
Glass Prints	48
Face Painting	50
Sarangi	52
Japanese Drum	54
Tweeters	56
Soap-Holder	58
Solitaire	60
Dinosaurs	62
Index	64

PHOTOGRAPH TREE

An illustrated family tree – keep it for yourself or give it as a birthday present to someone in your family.

You will need:

piece of cardboard
corrugated card
glue
net (e.g. supermarket vegetable bags)
green sugar paper
pieces of coloured tissue paper
family photographs
scissors

1 Cut the trunk and branches of the tree from corrugated card. Stick them on to the piece of cardboard.

2 Cut pieces of net to make bushy leaves. Stick them to the card.

3 Collect some photographs of members of your family (ask first). Cut out the heads and shoulders.

4 Cut a circle of tissue paper for each photograph. Pinch the middle of each so that it puckers slightly, then stick the photograph on to it.

5 Now glue each photograph on to your tree, putting the oldest members of your family at the top, and the youngest at the bottom.

6 Cut out small leaves from the sugar paper to stick round the photos.

Gift trees

Instead of cardboard, look for a real stick with several branches, then paint and press it into a plasticine base.

Now hang your photos from the branches.

For a tastier tree, use little bags of sweets instead of photos.

5

REPEATING PATTERNS

Islamic designs can be made by placing repeated shapes together. Fit them edge to edge and sometimes new shapes will appear in between.

You will need:

cardboard (cereal box)
coloured magazine
glue
paper
pencil
objects with interesting shapes
scissors

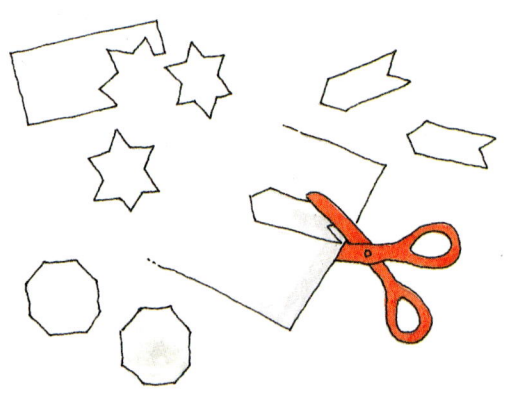

1 Make templates from part of a cardboard box by drawing around the shapes of some items found at home. We used a pastry cutter, an eraser, a plastic toy, and a cardboard box.

2 Cut out the shapes.

3 Place one of the templates on a page from a magazine. Draw around it. Then slide the shape along. Draw around it again and repeat 10 times.

4 Do the same thing again on a differently coloured page.

5 Cut the 12 shapes from one of the pages. Take the other page and cut out the areas in between.

6 Stick the pieces on to a piece of paper. Fit them neatly together without leaving any gaps.

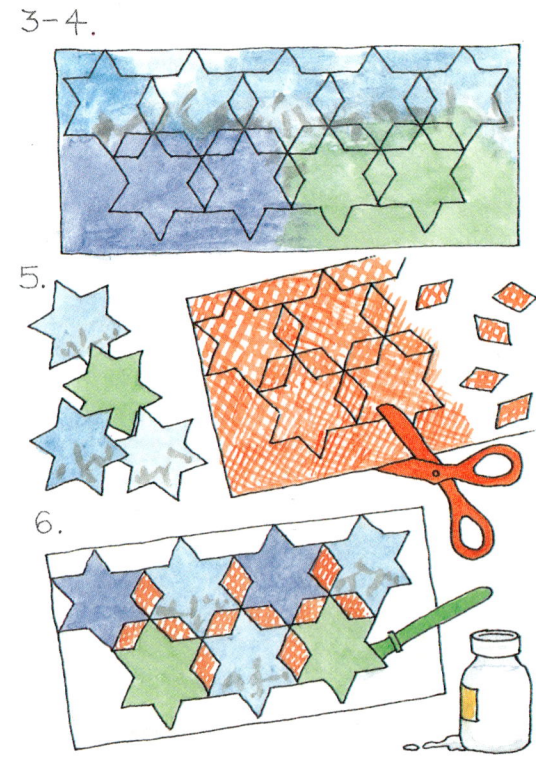

Decorate pots for your room by sticking on sheets of shapes.

JEWELLERY

Dress yourself up for a party with your own home-made jewellery.

You will need:

1 small cardboard tube
cotton thread
knitting needle
paint brush
paints
thin paper
paste/glue
string
vaseline

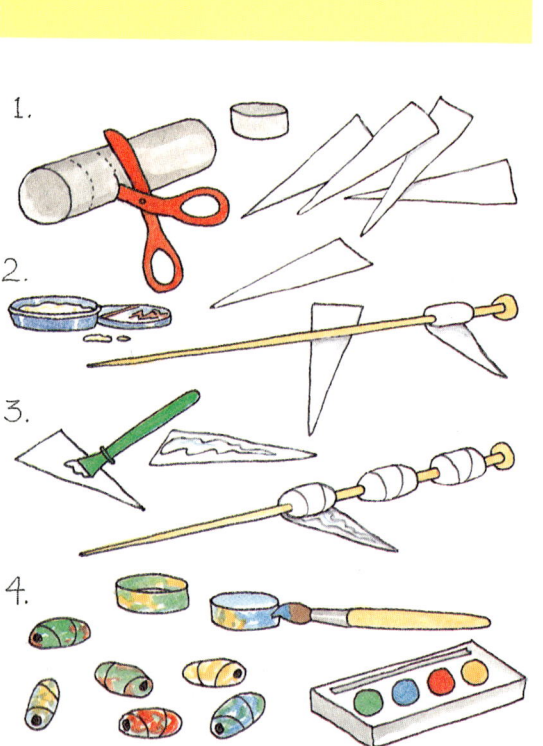

1 Cut the cardboard tube into rings and the paper into triangular strips, as shown.

2 Smooth a little vaseline over the needle.

3 To make the beads, brush the strips of paper with paste, then roll them around the needle, starting with the widest end each time. Leave to dry.

4 Remove the beads from the needle. Paint beads and rings in bright colours.

5.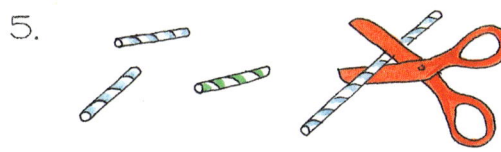

6.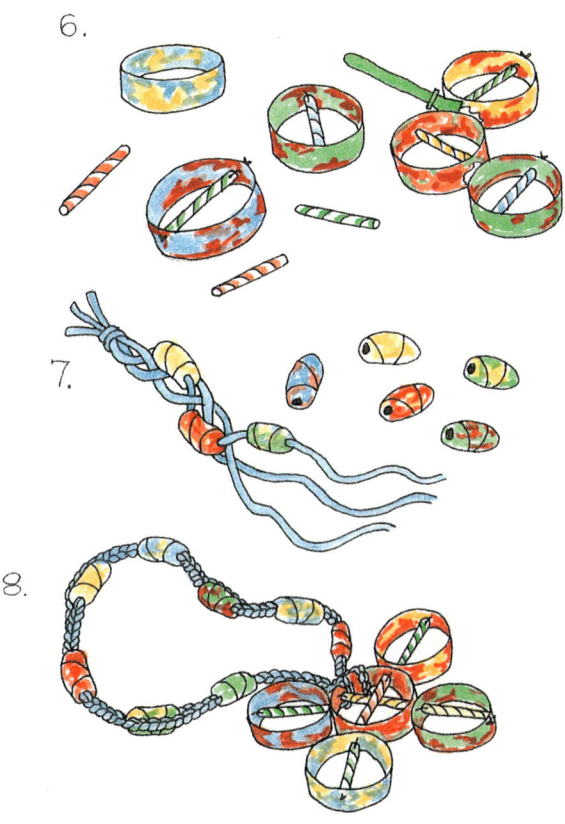

5 Cut a piece of straw to fit inside one of the rings. Do the same for the other rings.

6 Using thread, tie the straws into the rings then glue or tie the rings together.

7 Cut the string into three pieces. Plait them together, threading the beads into the plait, as shown.

8 Tie both ends of the plait to the rings.

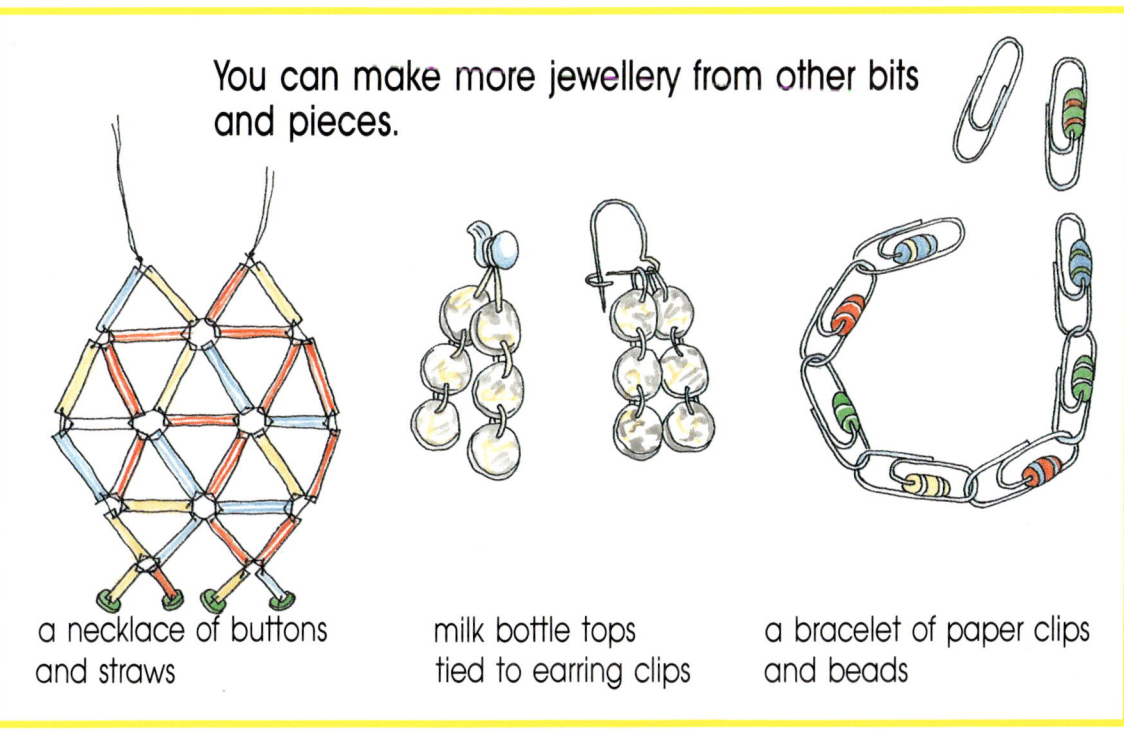

You can make more jewellery from other bits and pieces.

a necklace of buttons and straws

milk bottle tops tied to earring clips

a bracelet of paper clips and beads

9

BOTTLED HERBS

Grow fresh herbs for cooking in your own kitchen garden.

You will need:

charcoal
herb seeds or small plant
pebbles
clear plastic bottle
scissors
soil
400g yoghurt pot

1.

2.

3.

1 Cut the top from a 400g yoghurt container to make a pot about 10cm high.

2 Drop a layer of small pebbles, mixed with a little charcoal, into the bottom of the pot.

3 Pour in the compost to a depth of about 6cm.

4 Either sprinkle a few seeds into the pot and cover with a fine layer of soil, or make a hole in the middle of the soil and gently lower in the plant, pressing the earth firmly round the roots.

5 Water lightly.

6 Cut the bottom off the plastic bottle. Place the bottle over the pot and stand on a sunny window-sill.

7 Lift off the bottle to cut the herbs as you need them.

You can grow whole gardens in bottles.

Choose plants that are small and have pretty leaves. (Avoid flowering plants.) Water only once or twice a year.

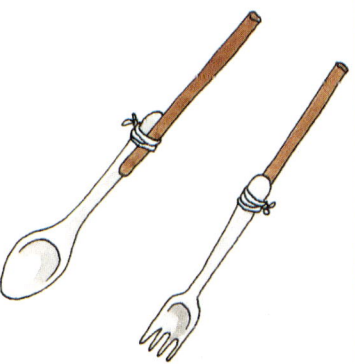

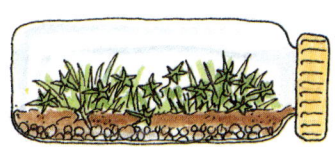

You may need to make special long-handled tools by tying sticks to a spoon and fork, as shown.

11

MINIATURE GARDEN

Landscape your own garden without going outside.

You will need:

cactus seeds or
   small plants
foil or small mirror
large ice-cream tub
small pebbles
2 plant pots
plastic bag
potting compost

 1.

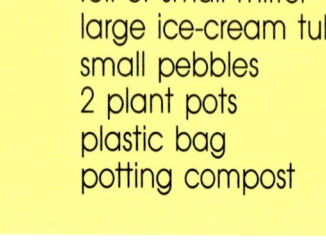

1 Cut a large ice-cream tub to about 4cm high.

2 Place 2 small pots at one end and fill with soil.

3 Lay the piece of foil, or mirror, on the soil, then sprinkle seeds around the edge and in the pots. Water lightly.

2.

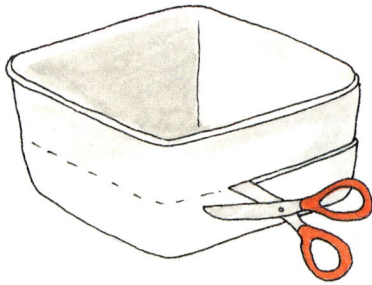

3.

4 Sprinkle some tiny stones or shells over the soil, then cover with a plastic bag.

5 Leave for a couple of months in a warm place keeping the soil moist.

6 Remove the plastic when the cactus plants are about 1cm high.

You can also use small ready-grown cacti, but wear rubber gloves when handling them. Gently squeeze the pot so that the roots come out with the earth round them, then pop into a hole in the soil. Press the earth firmly round the roots, then water well.

4 – 5.

6.

You can use any variety of containers for miniature gardens. Plant small flowers such as –

prayer plant

aluminium plant

pansies

maidenhair fern

primrose

small-leafed ivy

African violets

mother of thousands

13

BIRD NEST POTATOES

A supper dish that is filling and nutritious. To save time, bake the potato earlier and reheat it with the filling.

You will need:

butter
25g grated cheese
2 eggs
75ml milk
pepper
1 large potato

scrubbing brush

Set oven to 190 C, 375 F, gas mark 5

1 Scrub the potato clean, then prick the skin with a fork.

2 Bake for about 1 hour or until the potato feels soft when pressed.

3 Carefully cut in half. Scoop out the potato from the skin and place in a bowl.

4 Add milk, pepper, butter and mash well.

5 Fill both potato skins with the mixture and make a small hole in the middle of each.

6 Make patterns to look like twigs round the top with a fork, then sprinkle with grated cheese.

7 Break 1 egg into each hole and bake at 180 C, 350 F, gas mark 4 until set.

Try other fillings too

tomatoes

mushrooms

natural yoghurt

cottage cheese

baked beans

sweetcorn

prawns

spring onions

EASTERN DELIGHTS

Packed in their own special box, these sweets make a lovely Christmas present.

You will need:

1 tbsp apple juice
1 tbsp soft brown sugar
25g desiccated coconut
50g dried apple
25g dried apricots
25g dried dates
$\frac{1}{2}$ tsp ground cardamom
$\frac{1}{2}$ pint milk
1 tbsp milk powder
3 tbsps pudding rice
50g raisins
25g sultanas

blender (optional)

Sweet 1

1 Pour the milk into a saucepan and sprinkle in the milk powder. Stir well, then add the rice.

2 Bring to the boil, stirring all the time, then turn the heat down and simmer for 15 minutes.

3 Remove the pan from the cooker and add the sugar, cardamom and sultanas.

4 Pour the mixture into a bowl and leave to cool.

5 Roll into small balls in the palms of your hands then roll each ball in desiccated coconut.

Sweet 2

6 Remove date stones and chop the dates, apple and apricots and mix them with the raisins and apple juice in a large bowl. Mash them until they are as smooth as possible. (Use a blender if you have one.)

7 Shape into balls and roll in desiccated coconut.

To make a box for your sweets

Cut out a piece of card, as shown, and fold along the dotted lines. Stick together matching the letters.

Cut out a strip of card 30cm long.

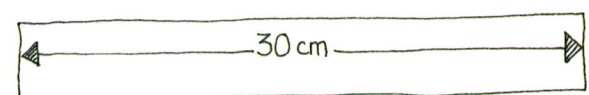

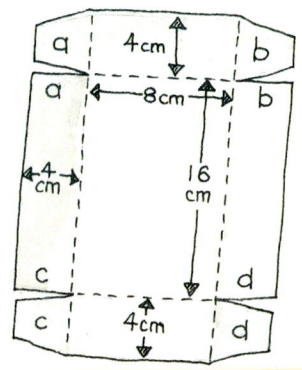

Stick the card round the box to make a handle.

Paint with brightly coloured patterns.

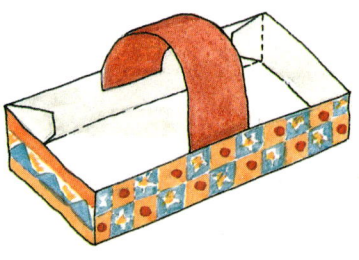

CHINESE DRAGON

A refreshing salad with a nutty flavour. Serve with lettuce and tomatoes.

You will need:

1 apple
1 carrot
½ cucumber
2 tbsps lemon juice
3 tbsps olive oil
50g peanuts
1 tbsp peanut butter
a pinch of pepper
2 radishes
50g raisins
1 spring onion

1. Wash the cucumber and halve it lengthways.

2. Scoop out the insides and place in a large bowl with the raisins and peanuts.

3. Wash the carrot, remove the top and grate the remainder into the bowl.

4. Wash the apple and chop into small pieces. Mix with the carrot.

5 Put the peanut butter in a small bowl. Gradually stir in the lemon juice, pepper and oil.

6 Mix well until smooth and creamy.

7 Add to the carrot mixture, stirring well, then heap into the two cucumber skins.

8 Peel the dry outer skin from the spring onion and slice in half lengthways. Wash the radishes. Remove the stalks and roots, then cut in half.

9 Make the dragon's tongue and eyes by placing a spring onion at the end of each piece of cucumber and adding half a radish on either side.

Here are some other ways to arrange salads.

Can you think of your own arrangements?

GREETINGS CARDS

Send cards with a difference this year. They can only be made by hand, so you rarely see anything like them in shops.

You will need:

card (24cm × 16cm)
embroidery silks
felt pens
needle
pencil
ruler
scissors

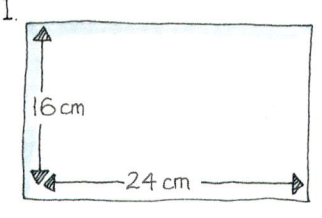 

1 Take a piece of card, 24cm by 16cm, and fold in half.

2 Draw a faint pencil line down the middle, then draw two triangles of the measurements shown.

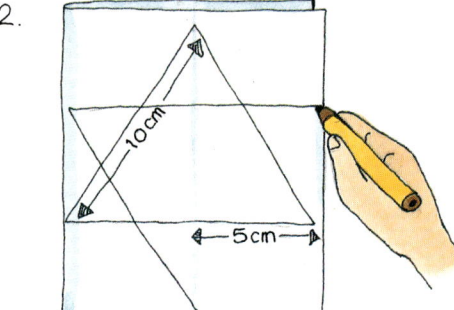

3 Mark 1cm intervals along the edges of the triangles. Prick a hole at each mark with a needle.

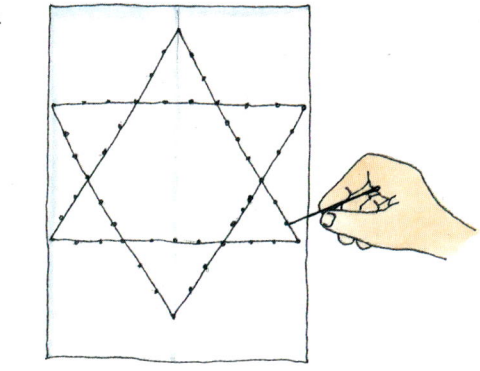

4 To sew the top triangle: thread a piece of silk up through the top hole (A) and down through (B), then up through (C) and down through (D). Continue this pattern as shown. Repeat, using a different coloured thread, for the other sides.

5 To sew the bottom triangle: follow the instructions in 4 above, using contrasting coloured threads.

6 Open the card and stick a piece of paper over the back of the design, to cover loose ends.

7 Cut the card into an interesting shape and write on your message.

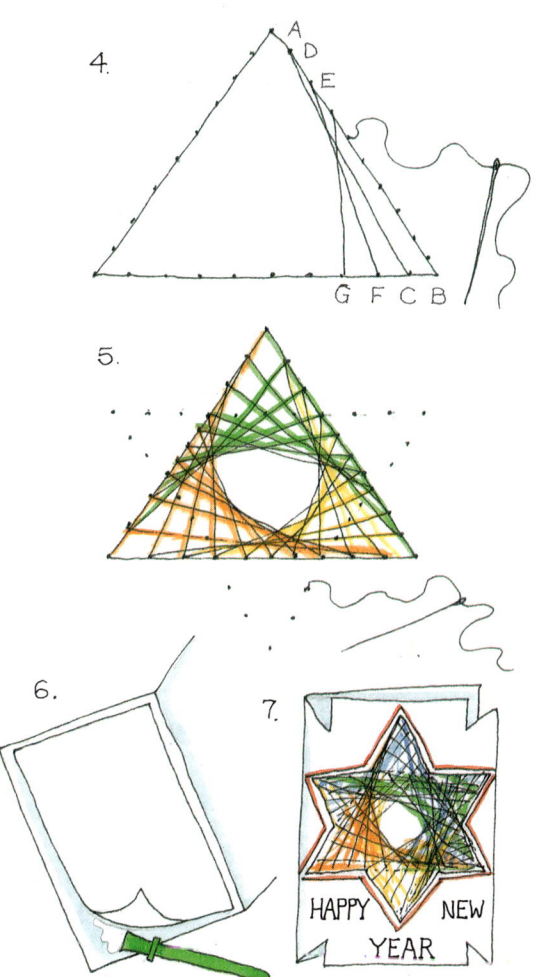

Here are some other designs you can try sewing.

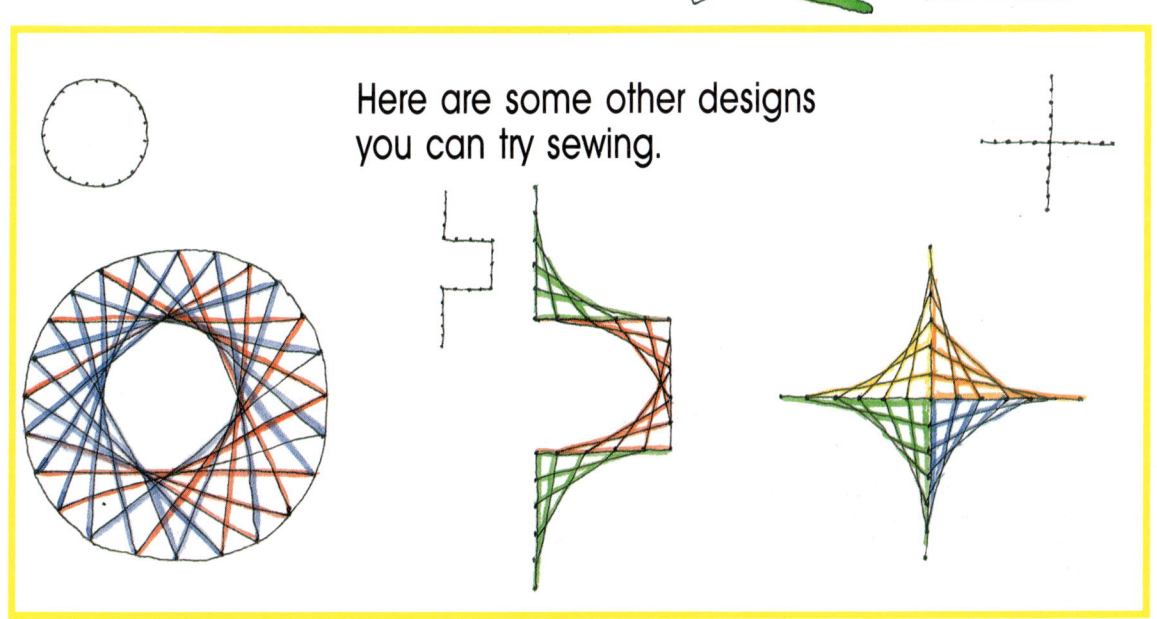

DESK TIDY

Collect all your pens and pencils together in one special holder, decorated in Mexican style.

You will need:

glue
jar
scissors
wools

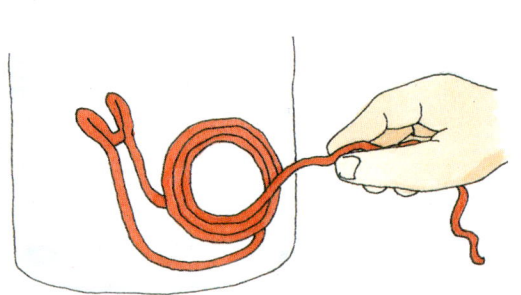

1 Paste some glue on a glass jar.

2 Press a length of wool on to the glue to make the outline of a snail.

3 Fill in the outline by coiling the wool towards the centre. Then cut off the extra wool.

4 Repeat, using the other shapes shown. Press the strands of wool closely together so that no glass shows.

5 Leave to dry.

6 Fill in the spaces between the shapes in the same way. Continue until the whole jar is covered.

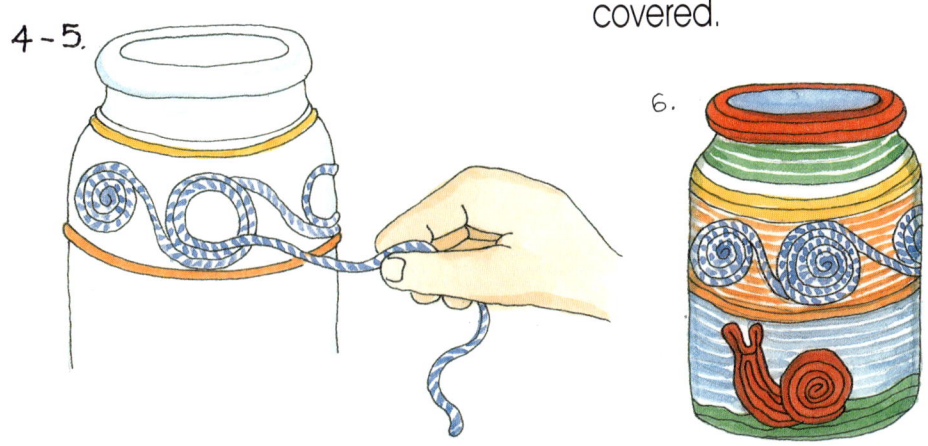

4 - 5.

6.

To make Christmas decorations.

Smear an inflated balloon with Vaseline. Cut 30cm lengths of string. Dip them into the glue, then wind round the balloon.

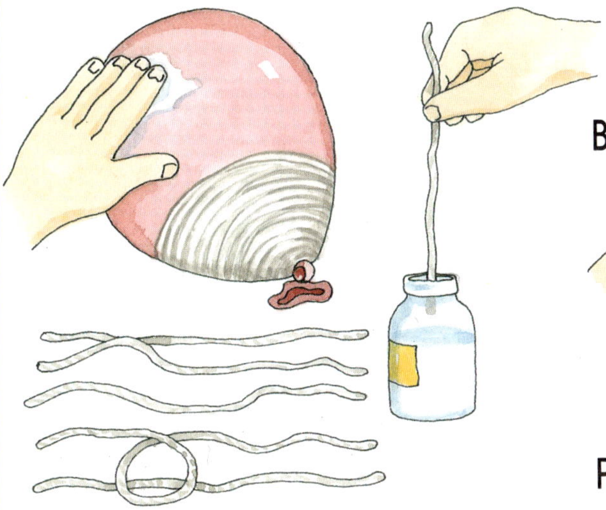

Hang to dry.

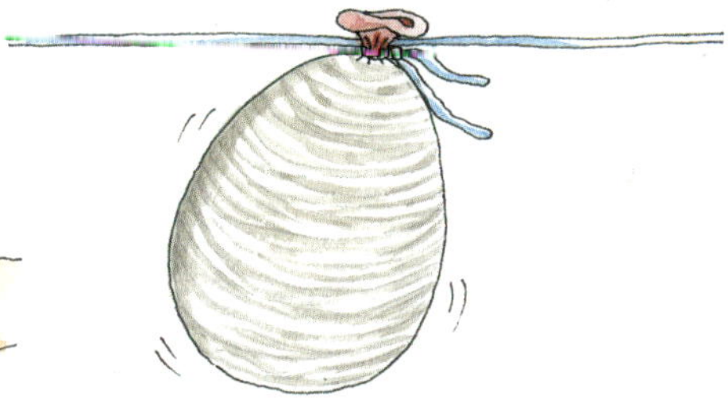

Burst the balloon.

Paint the ball gold or silver.

23

FABRIC PAINTING

Make you own designer vest or T-shirt and impress your friends.

You will need:

card
fabric paints/brushes
black felt pen
iron and clean cloth
pins
T-shirt or vest

CAUTION: irons can be dangerous. Ask an adult to help you make this item.

1 Take a piece of card smaller than the front of your T-shirt.

2 Draw your design on to the card using a black felt pen.

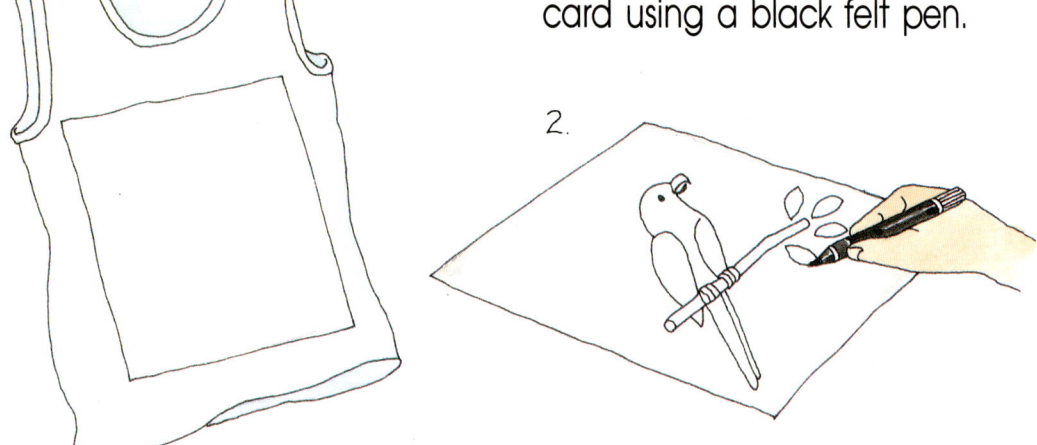

3.

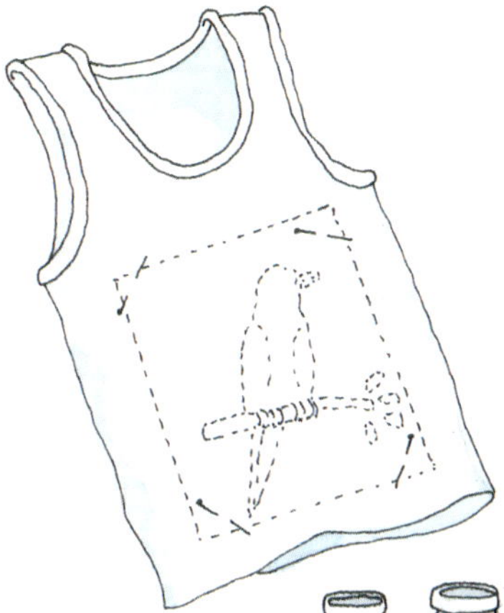

4-5.

3 Place the card inside the T-shirt so that the design shows through the front. Pin into place.

4 Carefully paint your picture. Use thick paint, applying it with short strokes or dabs.

5 Leave to dry.

6 Remove the card, then cover with a clean cloth and iron.

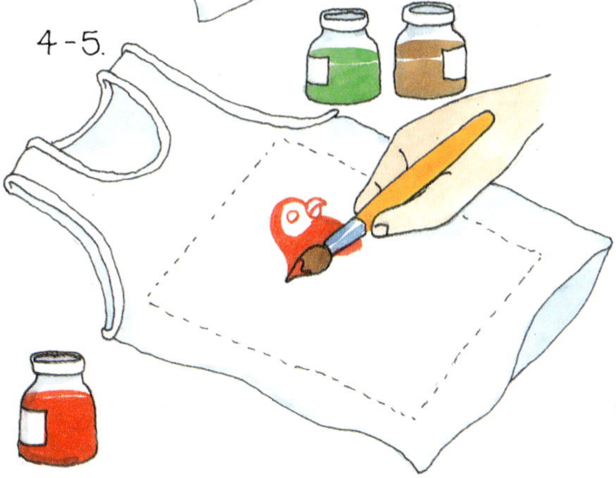

6.

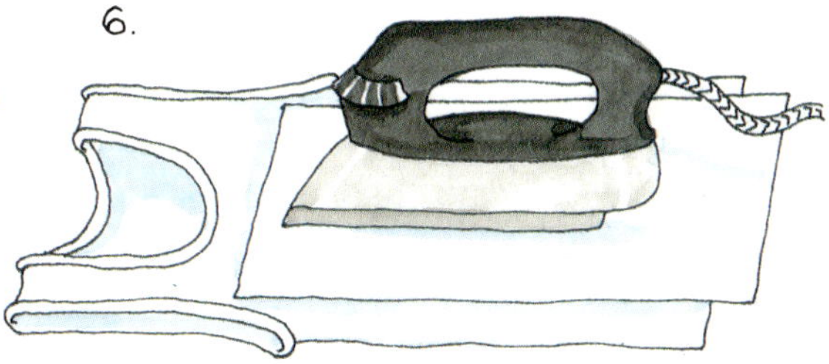

Designs painted on small squares of material can be used as patches, or to decorate a bag.

25

TIE AND DYE SCARF

Tie and dye is a quick, simple way to make patterns on fabric. It is practised all over the world. Sling the scarves round your neck, or tie at the waist.

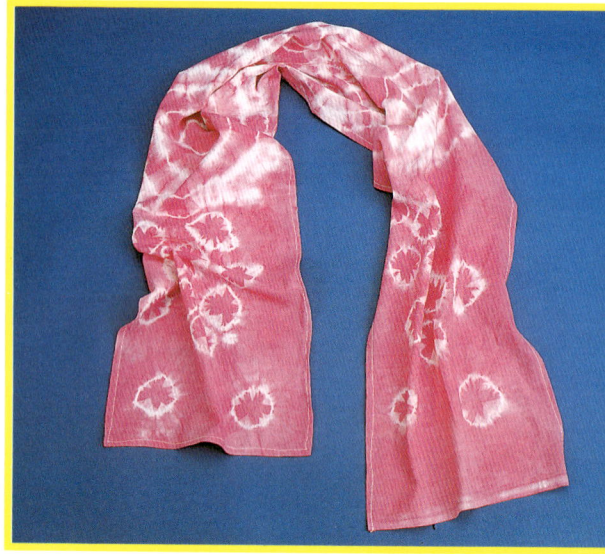

You will need:

old bucket
length of cotton material
cold water dye
fixative
pebbles or marbles
scissors
stick
string

1 Take a scarf-length piece of cotton (a piece from an old sheet is fine).

2 Tie the scarf in one, or several of these ways
   – tie a pebble or marble into the cotton (A)
   – twist the cotton round, then tie it in several places as shown (B)
   – pleat the material and tie (C).

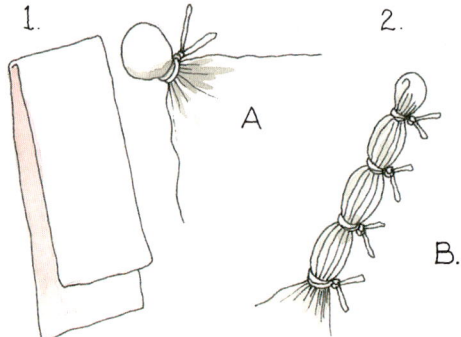
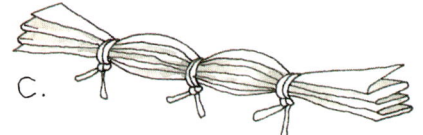
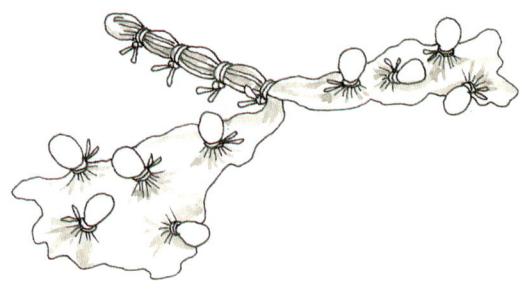

Be sure that all your ties are tight.

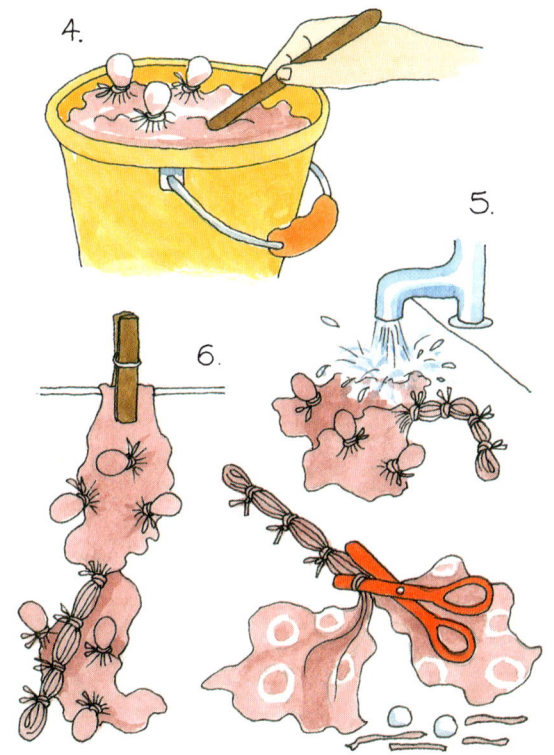

3 Mix the dye, following the instructions on the packet. Add a fixative so the colour does not wash out.

4 Put the scarf into the dye and leave until the colour is twice as dark as you want.

5 Rinse thoroughly in cold water.

6 Leave to dry, then remove the ties.

7 This process can be repeated with a second, darker colour.

Old cotton shirts and skirts can be given a new lease of life with tie and dye.

MOVING PICTURES

When you watch a cartoon, you are actually seeing hundreds of separate pictures flashing in front of your eyes. The pictures change so quickly that they trick your eyes into seeing the cartoon characters move. Your eyes play a similar trick when you look at this spinning disc.

You will need:

card (20×20cm)
a circular object to draw round
coloured pens or paints
pencil
scissors
string (120cm)

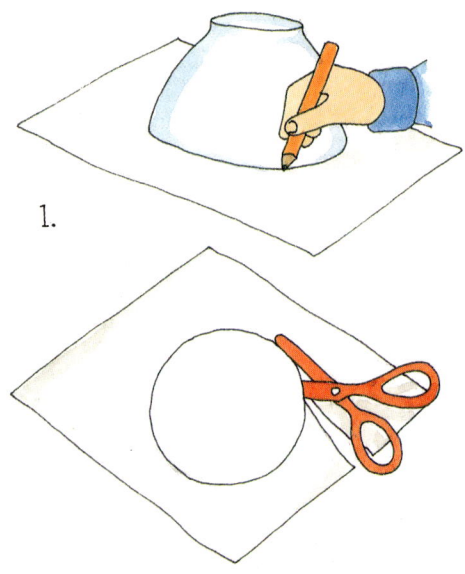

1.

1 Cut a circle about 15cm in diameter from a piece of card.

2 Make two holes on either side.

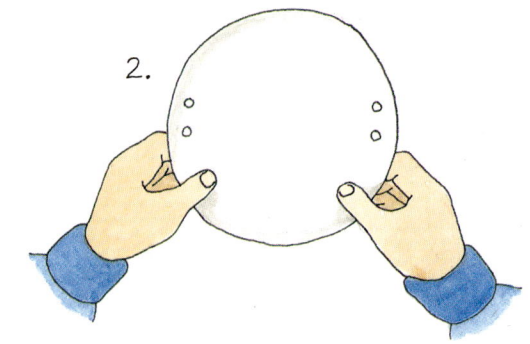

2.

28

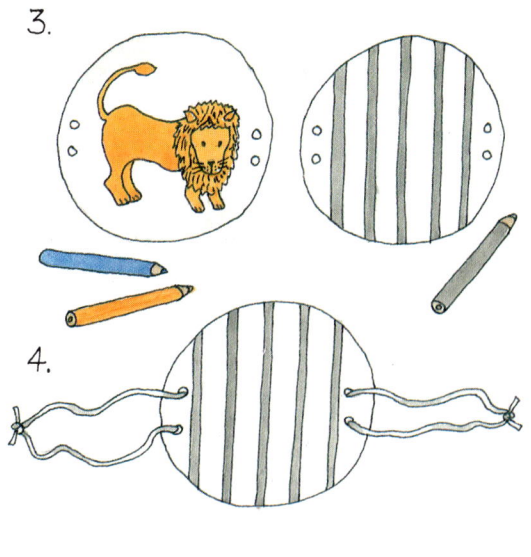

3 Draw a lion on one side and the bars of his cage on the other.

4 Thread a piece of string through the holes on either side. Knot the ends.

5 Hold one end of the string still and wind the other round to twist the string. Then pull sharply on the string so that the card spins. It will look as if the lion is safely back in his cage.

More moving pictures:

Fold a piece of paper in half. Draw a seated figure on the top half.

Now draw the same figure underneath, standing up. Roll a pencil up in the top 'page'. Roll it backwards and forwards and watch the figure move.

WINDOW PICTURE

Some papers allow the light to shine through them when you hold them up to the window. See how the light brightens up this picture.

You will need:

card (30×20cm)
cellophane sweet wrappers
glue
scissors
thin coloured plastic
white and coloured tissue paper

1.

1 Collect a variety of see-through papers, such as sweet wrappers, coloured tissue paper, crisp packets, etc.

2 Cut a rectangle from the centre of a piece of card to leave a frame.

3 Stick a large piece of white tissue paper over the frame and trim the edges.

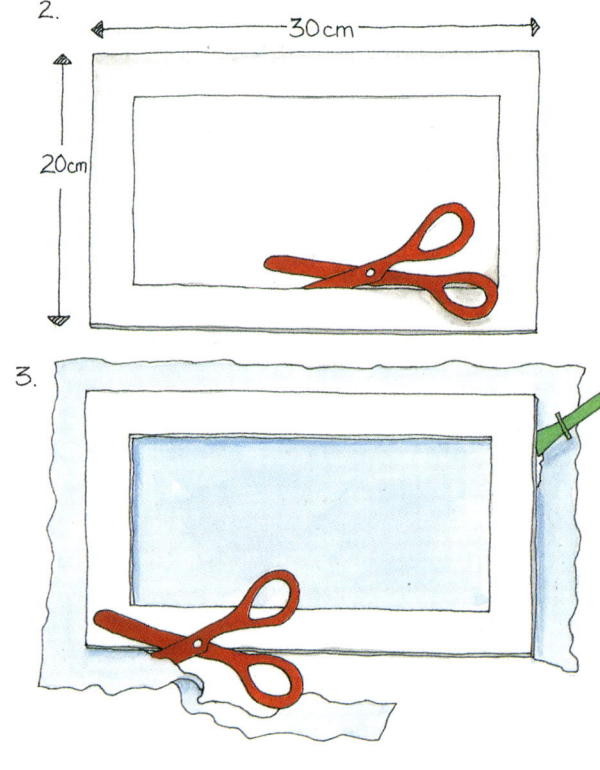

4 Cut a variety of insect bodies, wings, antennae and legs from the pieces of see-through paper. (Make them as real or fantastic as you wish.)

5 Smear a little glue onto the tissue paper, then gently stick the pieces into place.

6 Leave to dry. Display on a window so the light shines through.

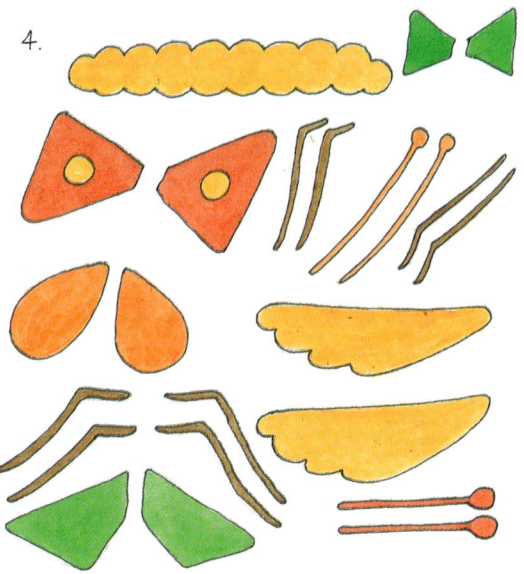

Underwater scenes make interesting window pictures. Perhaps you can experiment with a mixture of see-through and non see-through papers.

ACROBAT

This dancing stick puppet can be used as part of a puppet show. I have made an acrobat, but you may like to make some characters of your own.

You will need:

card
coloured pens or paints
8 paper fasteners
pencil
pin
scissors
stick (30cm)
sticky tape

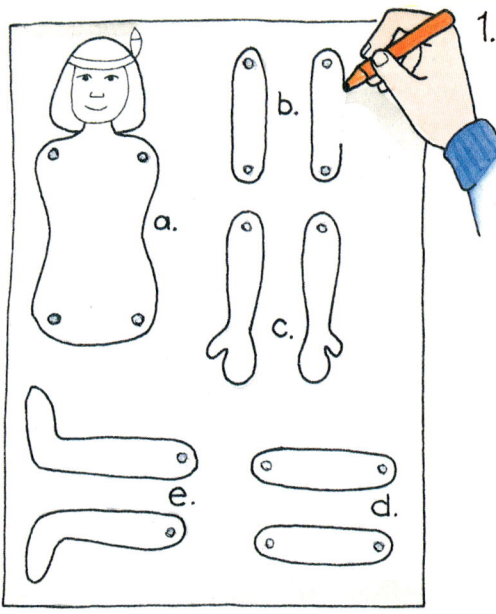

1 Draw the parts of the acrobat onto card:
   a head and body with large shoulders and hips
   b two upper arms
   c two hands and lower arms
   d two upper legs
   e two lower legs with feet
   Mark an 'O' on all the joints.

2 Paint in bright colours, then cut out.

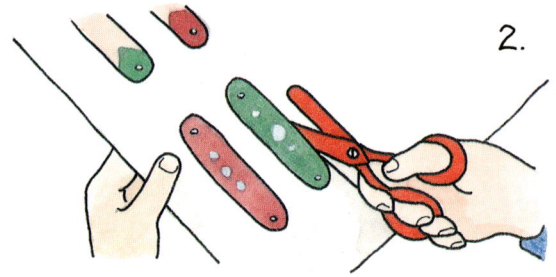

3.

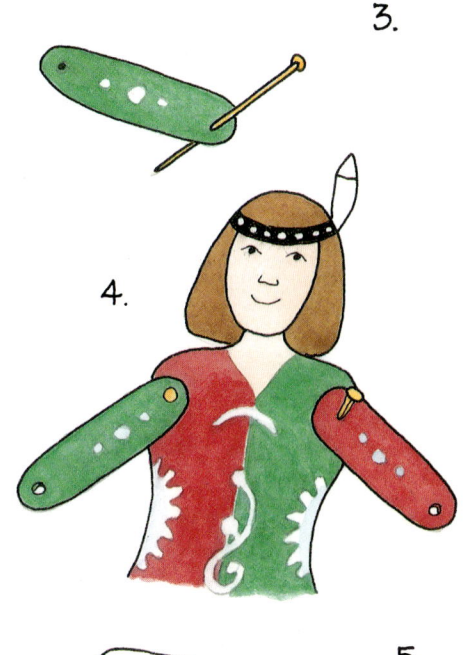
4.

5.

3 Use a pin to make a hole at the points marked 'O'.

4 Join the upper arms to the shoulders with a paper fastener. Join the upper legs to the hips.

5 Join the hands to the arms, and the feet to the legs.

6 Tape a stick to the back.

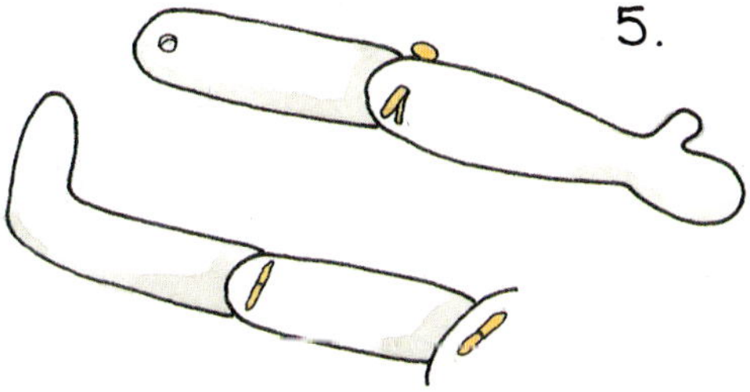

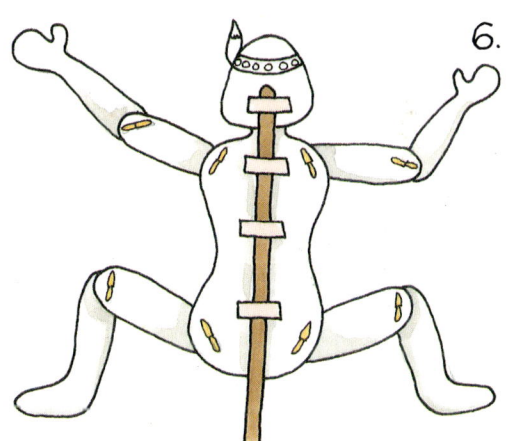
6.

You can make several acrobats and arrange them to form a frieze.

33

CHINESE DRAGON

In China, the New Year is celebrated with dragon dances. You can easily make your own dragon puppet to dance with.

You will need:

glue
scissors
2 sticks (30cm)
sticky tape
sugar paper (100×50cm)

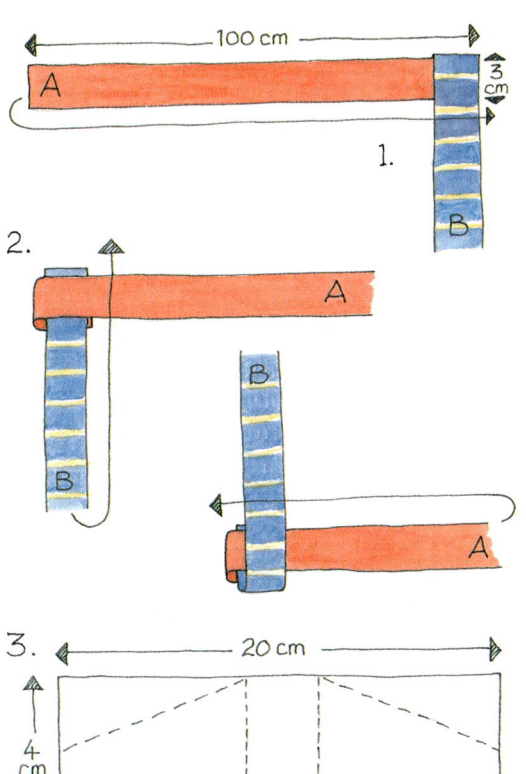

1 Cut two strips of paper, each about 100cm long, and place one over the other at right angles.

2 Fold piece A back over B, then fold B over A and continue folding the strips one after the other. When the strips are finished, fasten the ends with sticky tape.

3 To make the head, cut out a rectangle of paper and fold along the imaginary dotted lines.

34

4 To make the eyes, screw up two small pieces of paper and glue them to the top of the head. Glue the head to one end of the body.

5 Cut out a long paper tail and glue it to the other end.

6 Tape the sticks to the body as shown.

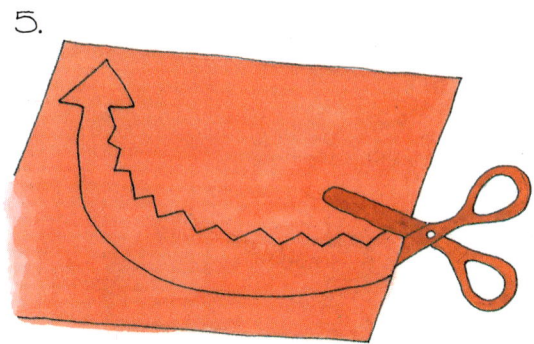

Some Christmas decorations are made by weaving paper in this way. See if you can make some to brighten up your room.

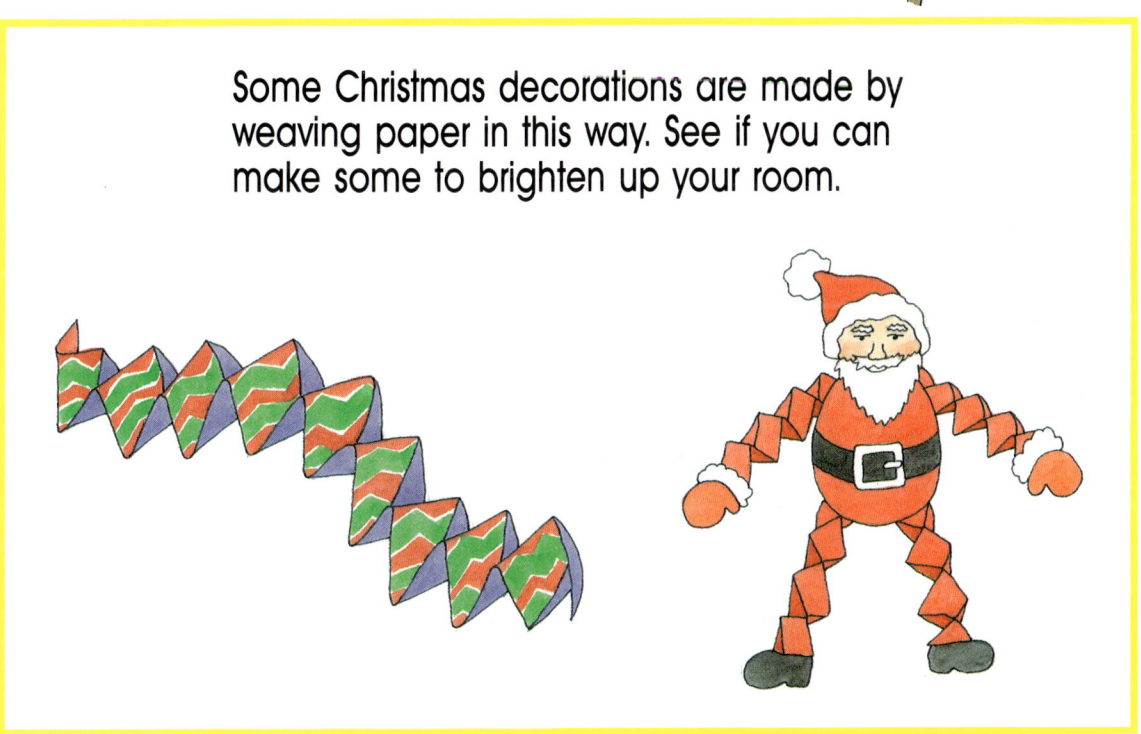

35

ACROBATIC ANGLER

Watch your little fisherwoman dance on the edge of your table as she struggles to land her catch.

You will need:

card
cocktail stick
coloured pens
matchbox
paste
Plasticine
pliers
scissors
small stick
table-tennis ball
wire
wool

1 Cut two sticks, each 2cm longer than the matchbox.

2 Make two holes in the bottom of the matchbox and push the sticks into the holes.

3 Push one end of the cocktail stick into the table-tennis ball and the other end into the top of the matchbox.

4 Paint a face on the ball and stick on wool for hair. Decorate the matchbox as a body.

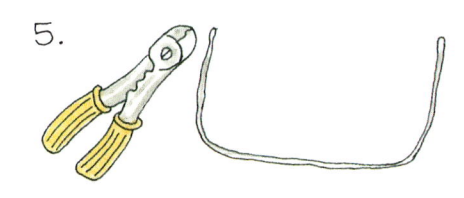

5 Cut a piece of wire, 30cm long, and bend it into a 'U' shape.

6 Push one end through the middle of the matchbox. Stand the figure on the edge of the table and balance by fixing Plasticine to the bottom of the wire as shown.

7 Stick paper arms from the matchbox to the wire.

8 Cut out two paper fish and stick over the Plasticine.

How does it work?

An object which is bottom heavy is less likely to fall over than one which is top heavy. The Plasticine underneath the fisherwoman weighs her down and helps her to balance.

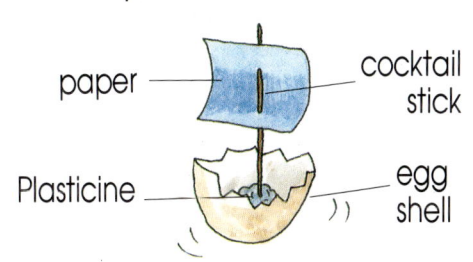

Make other balancing toys.

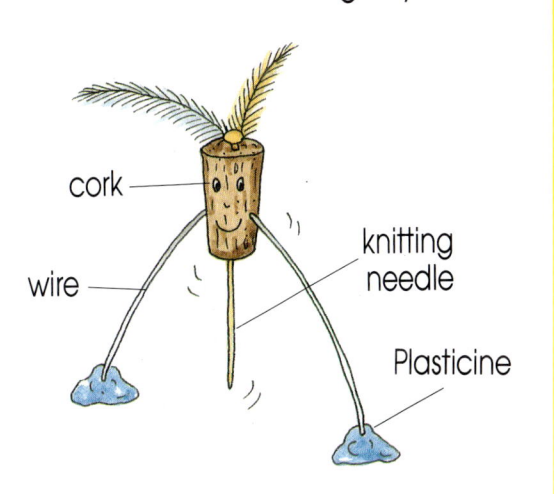

DIVING OCTOPUS

Fascinate your friends with this 'pet octopus' which dives to the bottom of the bottle at your command.

You will need:

coloured plastic
coloured plastic bag
jug
paste
pen cap (without holes or cracks)
plastic bottle
Plasticine
scissors

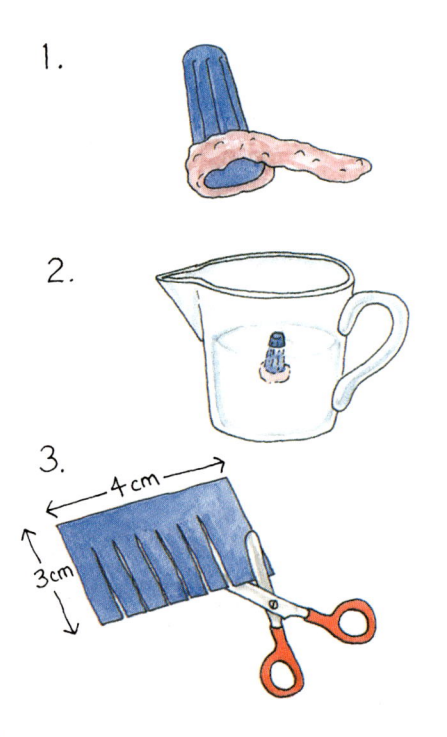

1.

2.

3.

1 Press a ring of Plasticine to the rim of a pen cap, making sure you do not fill the hole.

2 Place the cap in a jug of water so that it just floats above the surface. (You may need to remove or add more Plasticine.)

3 Cut a rectangle of coloured plastic 3cm × 4cm from the bag, then make a fringe, cutting from the bottom almost to the top as shown.

38

4 Tie the plastic round the cap and over the Plasticine.

5 Cut strands of weed and the outline of a submarine from other pieces of plastic, then stick to the outside of the bottle.

6 Fill the bottle to the brim with water, lower in the pen cap and tightly screw on the top.

7 Make the octopus dive to the bottom by squeezing the bottle.

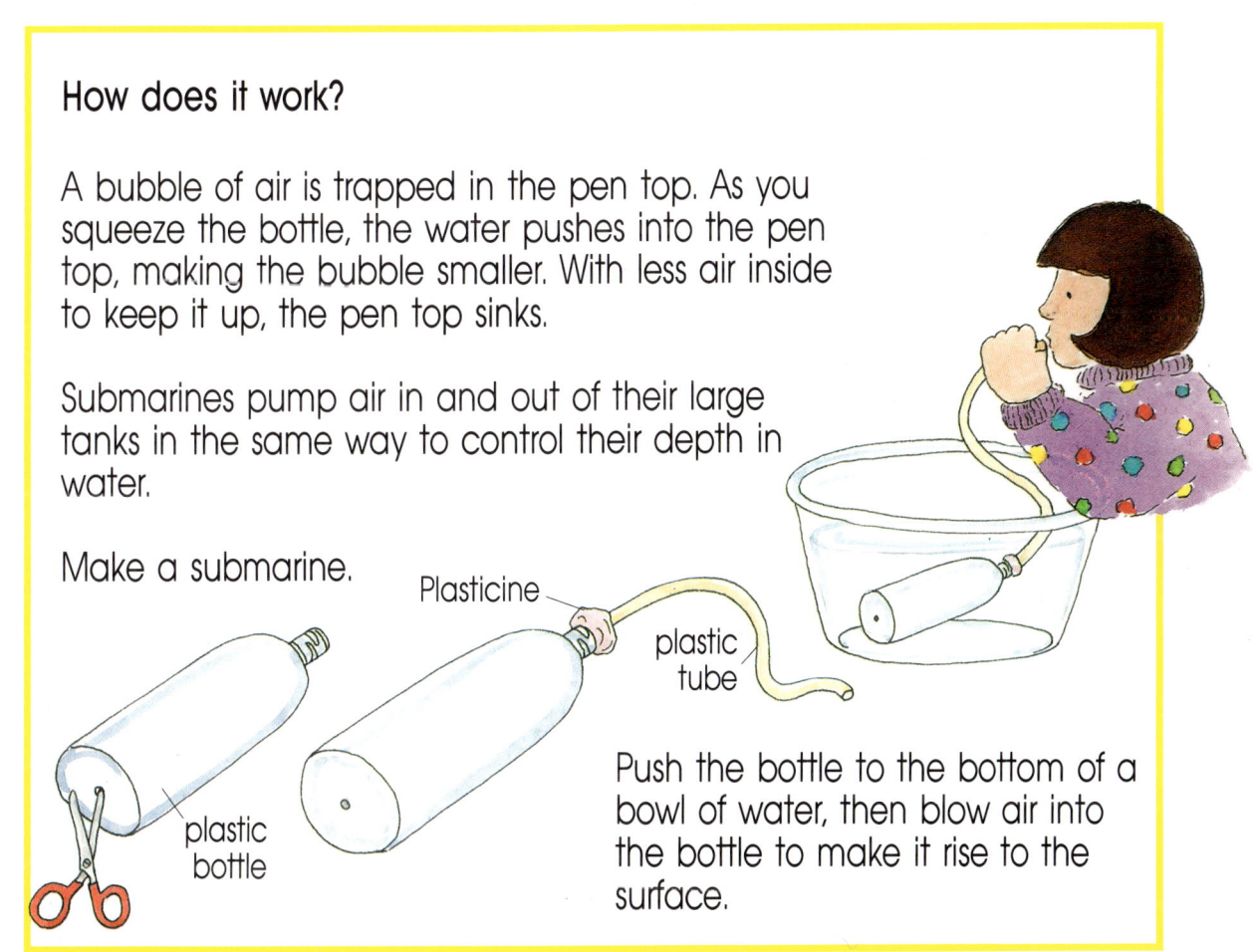

How does it work?

A bubble of air is trapped in the pen top. As you squeeze the bottle, the water pushes into the pen top, making the bubble smaller. With less air inside to keep it up, the pen top sinks.

Submarines pump air in and out of their large tanks in the same way to control their depth in water.

Make a submarine.

Push the bottle to the bottom of a bowl of water, then blow air into the bottle to make it rise to the surface.

HELICOPTER

A toy for outside (so you won't break any windows). As you pull on the string the helicopter will fly up into the air.

You will need:

2 buttons
card
cotton reel
glue
paints or pens
pencil
ruler
sticky tape
string
thin stick or cane

1 Cut a piece of card into the shape shown.

2 Stick buttons to the ends of two opposite blades. Stick the cotton reel to the centre.

3 Decorate with paints or pens.

4.

4 Wind the string round the cotton reel from the bottom to the top. (It must be wound this way or the helicopter will not fly upwards.)

5 Bend the blades gently along the dotted lines so they twist and hang down slightly.

6 Put the cotton reel on a stick and pull the string down sharply.

5.

6.

How does it work?

As the blades spin, the air rushing over the curved top has further to go than the air underneath. This weakens the air pressure above the blades which are pushed up from beneath.

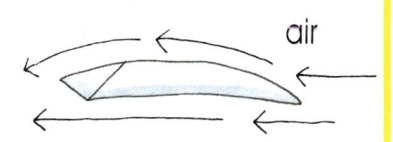

air

Make a paper aeroplane.

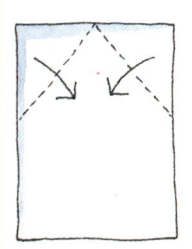

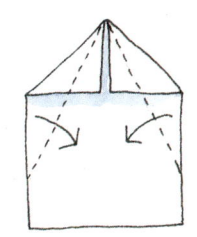

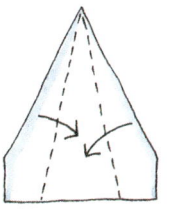

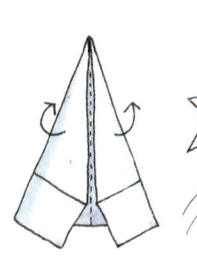

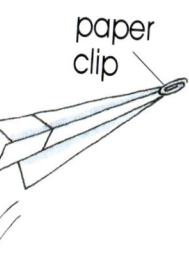

paper clip

fold to centre   fold to centre   turn over   fold to centre   fold in half   open up wings

41

DART AND LAUNCHER

This dart's streamlined shape makes it shoot forwards at great speed. See how far it will travel.

You will need:

card
elastic band
paints or pens
paper
paste
3 pins
scissors
sheet of polystyrene
small cardboard box

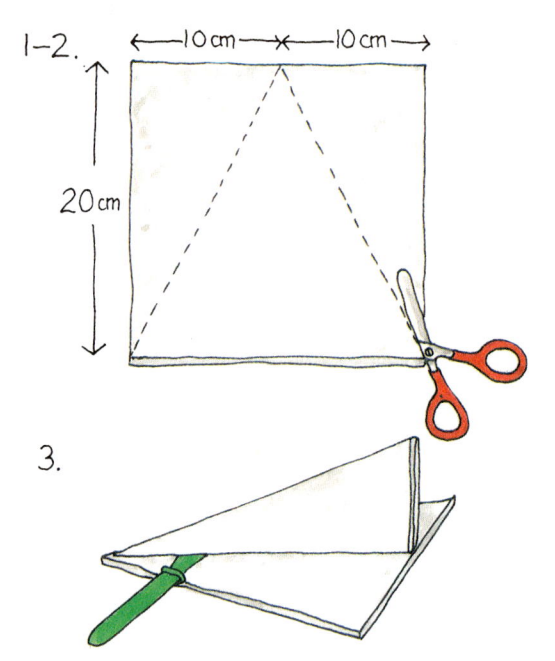

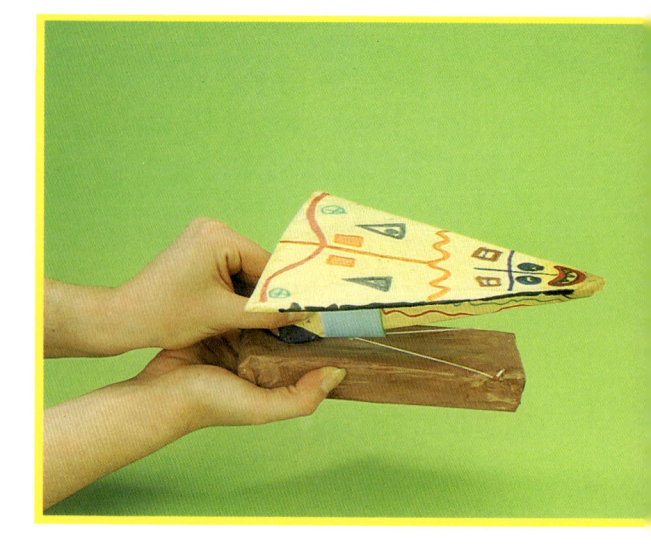

1 Cut a 20cm square from a sheet of polystyrene.

2 Cut off two corners to make a triangle as shown.

3 Stick one of the corner pieces to the centre of the triangle in an upright position. Cover with paper.

4 Cut a strip of card 2cm × 6cm, fold in half and stick over the top of the upright.

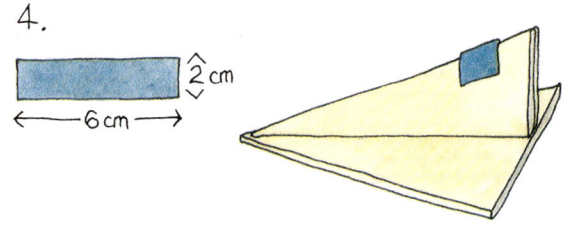

5.

6.

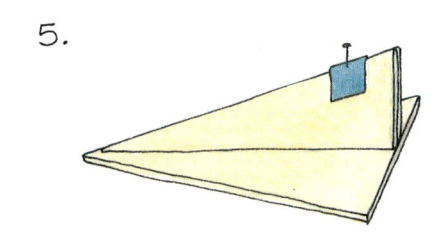

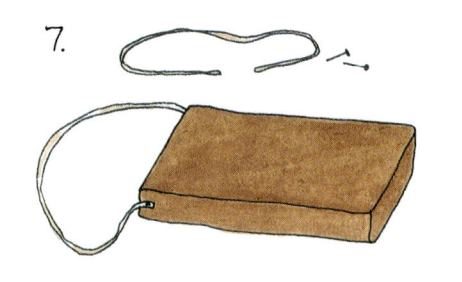

7.

5 Press a pin into the card.

6 Decorate with paints or pens.

7 To make the launcher, cut open an elastic band and pin each end to the top of a cardboard box as shown.

8 Launch the dart by holding the pin against the elastic and pulling it back. When the elastic is fully stretched, let go of the dart.

8.

How does it work?

When the elastic is pulled backwards it is being stretched by force. When it is released it returns suddenly to its normal shape, forcing the dart forwards.

Make a cannon launcher with a paper foil cannonball. Use the hook to pull the elastic down the tube, then release to fire.

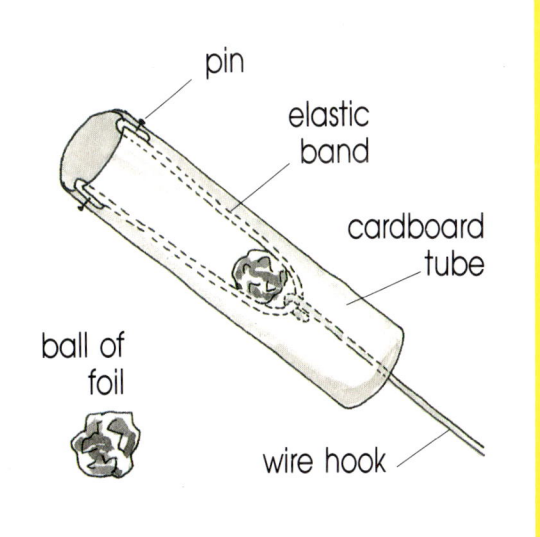

pin
elastic band
cardboard tube
ball of foil
wire hook

GIFT BOXES

Home-made gift boxes will make the presents you give your friends and family extra special.

You will need:

2 sheets of card
 (each 420mm × 297mm)
poster or powder paints
pencil and ruler
scissors
string

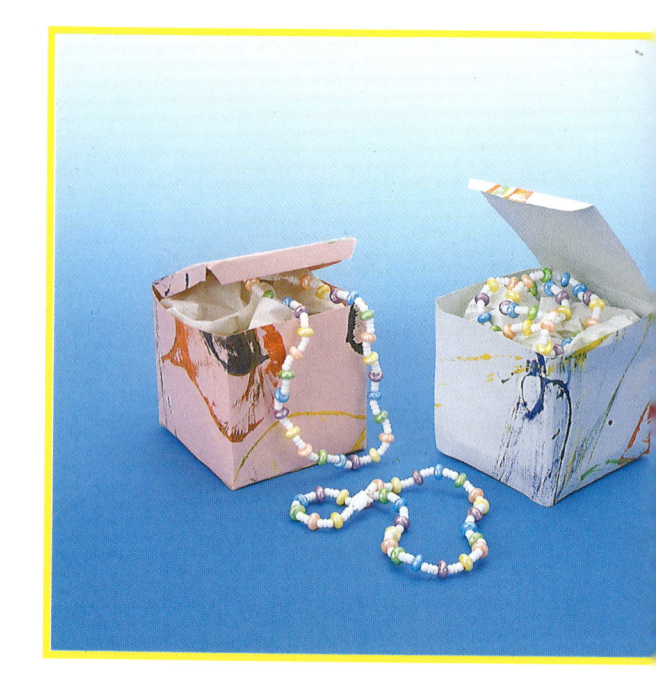

1.

1 Cut three pieces of string, each about 30cm long.

2 Dip each piece into a different-coloured pot of paint, then lay carefully on a sheet of card, allowing one end of each to hang over the edge.

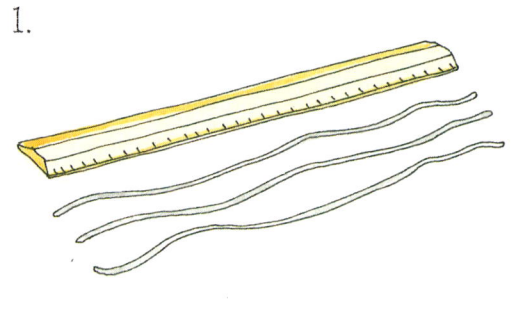

2.

44

3 Place the second sheet of card on top.

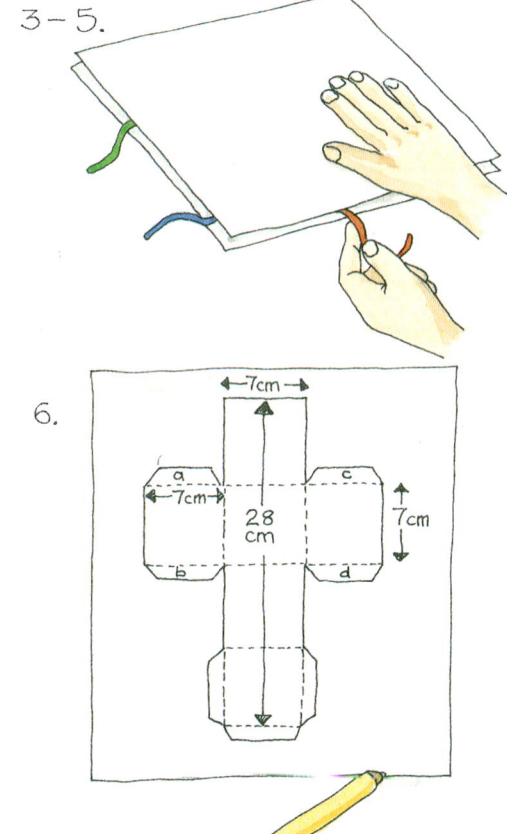

3-5.

6.

4 Holding the top card firmly in place, slowly pull out each piece of string so that the paint smudges.

5 Carefully separate the two pieces of card and leave to dry.

6 Draw six squares and 'flaps' as shown, on the back of the cards.

7 Cut along the solid lines ——— Fold along the dotted lines........

8 Stick the flaps (a b c d) to the sides to make the boxes.

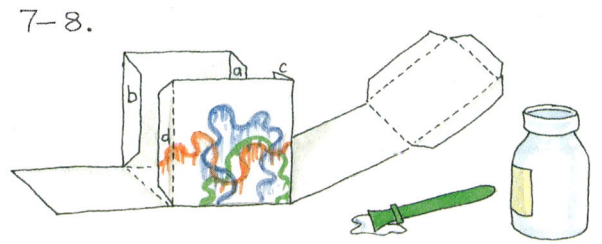

7-8.

You can use other things besides brushes for painting. Try some of these –

string a piece of card a sponge an old comb

a feather

FISH MOBILE

Hang this colourful mobile in front of an open window and it will catch the light as it spins round.

You will need:

cotton thread
blue packaging paper or tissue
glue
paintbrush
pliers
2-ply kitchen paper
poster paints
scissors
sponge
a stick or cane
wire

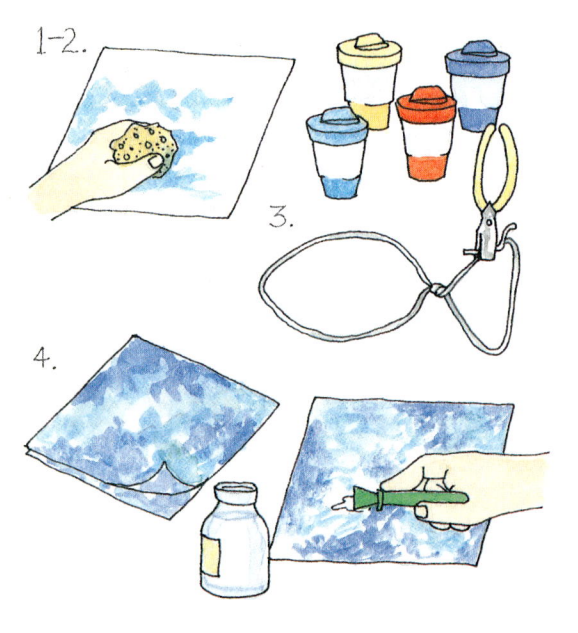

1 Dampen a piece of kitchen paper with a wet sponge, then carefully dab on poster paint.

2 Hang up to dry.

3 Bend a piece of wire into the shape of a fish. (Use pliers to twist the two ends together.)

4 Carefully pull apart the paper to make two pieces, and spread glue over one piece.

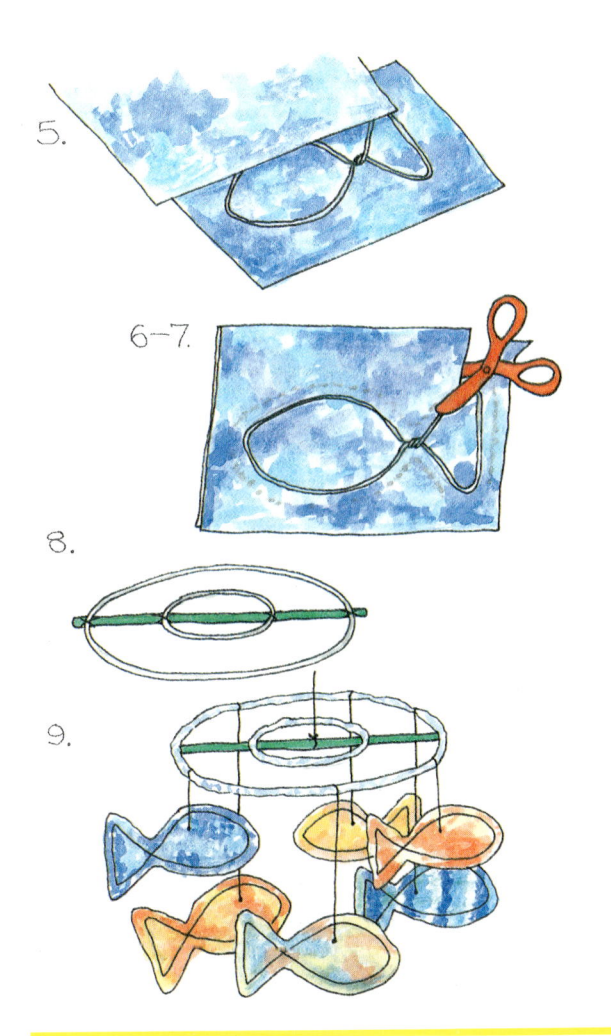

5 Place the wire fish on to the glue, then stick the second piece of paper on top. Leave to dry.

6 Cut round the shape of the fish about 1cm from the wire.

7 Then make five more fish in the same way.

8 Make two circles of wire and bind them to the stick as shown. Hang the fish from the wire with the cotton thread.

9 Wind blue tissue paper or plastic bubbly packaging material around the wire. Small pieces of Plasticine can be hidden in the tissue to help balance the mobile.

Make a stained glass window.

Cut a frame from black paper or card and stick on kitchen tissue, coloured in the same way as above. To get the best effect, hold up to the light or stick to a window.

47

GLASS PRINTS

Make an attractive box for your paints and brushes using these eye-catching glass prints.

You will need:

empty cardboard box
  (e.g. a shoe box)
kitchen paper
paintbrush, cardboard comb
  or other paint spreader
poster paints
sheet of glass or plastic
sheet of paper

1 Splodge the paint thickly on to the glass or plastic using a large paintbrush.

2 Spread the paint with your fingers, with paintbrushes or with pieces of cardboard.
(If necessary, wipe some paint away with a piece of kitchen tissue.)

48

3.

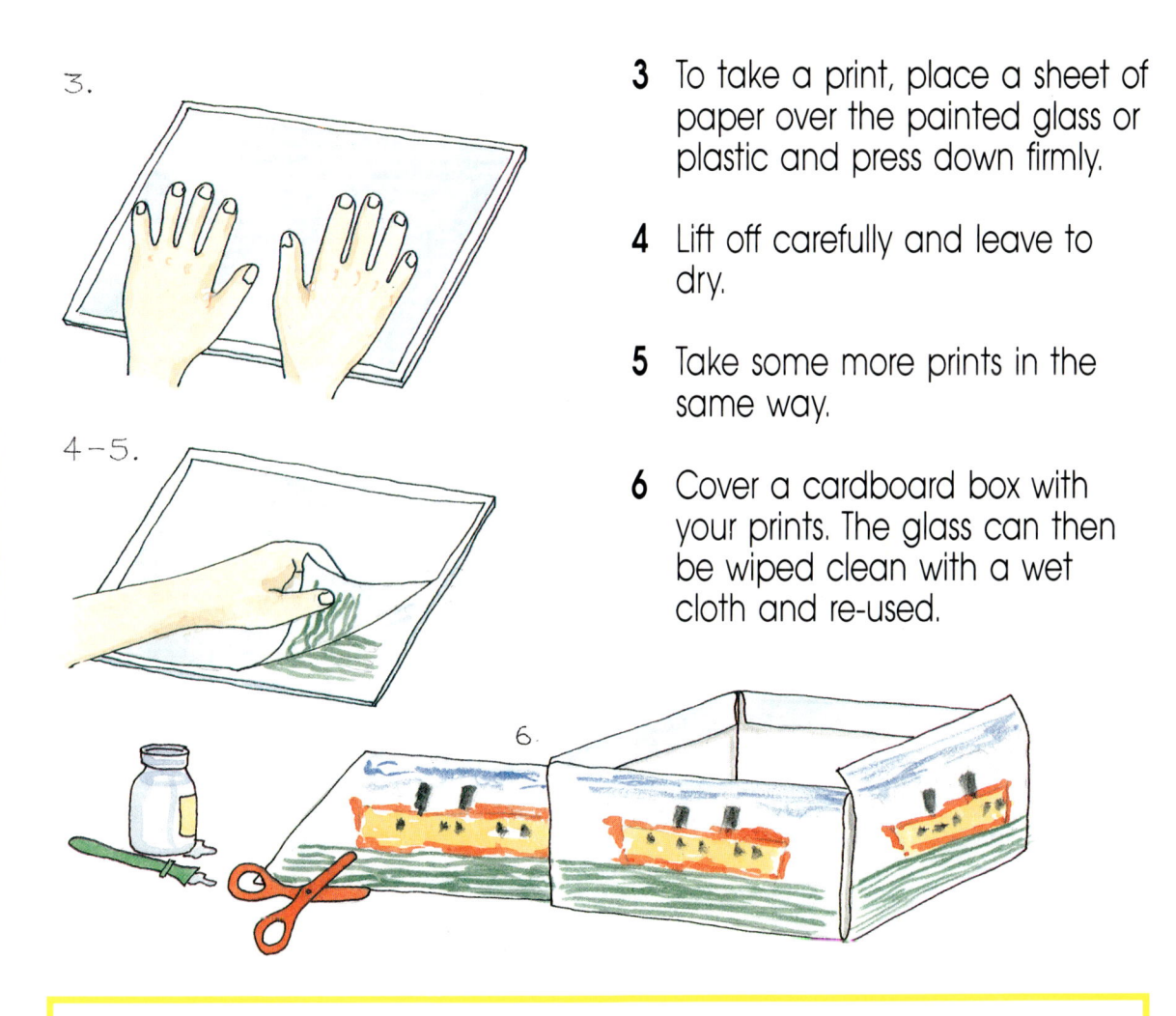

4-5.

6.

3 To take a print, place a sheet of paper over the painted glass or plastic and press down firmly.

4 Lift off carefully and leave to dry.

5 Take some more prints in the same way.

6 Cover a cardboard box with your prints. The glass can then be wiped clean with a wet cloth and re-used.

Use a wax crayon to draw a picture on the glass, and then spread paint thickly over the top. Take a print.

FACE PAINTING

All over the world, people paint their bodies for decoration – some to look attractive, others for special occasions like fairs, carnivals or ceremonies. This recipe tells you how to make face paints for you and your friends.

You will need:

cheese grater
cooker
25g cornflour
mixing bowl
thin paintbrush
non-toxic powder paints
saucepan
sieve
half a 125g bar of soap
spoon
250ml water
3 yoghurt pots

CAUTION: boiling water can scald. Ask an adult to help.

1. Mix the cornflour with a little water to make a smooth paste.

2. Pour the rest of the water into a saucepan and stir in the paste. Bring to the boil, stirring well, then remove from the heat.

3. Grate the soap into flakes.

4 Drop them into the hot water, a few at a time, and stir until they dissolve.

5 Pour the mixture through a sieve and leave to cool.

6 Divide the mixture between the yoghurt pots, add a teaspoon of different coloured powder paint to each, and mix well.

7 Paint some of the simple designs shown here, using a thin paintbrush.

The paints will wash off easily, but keep some tissues handy in case you make a mistake.

Mehndi

Henna powder, mixed into a paste with lemon juice and drops of warm water, is used in Pakistan and India to decorate the palms of the hands. You can try this but, be warned, the colour lasts for a week.

Alternatively, you could try out some patterns on a cardboard cut-out of your hand.

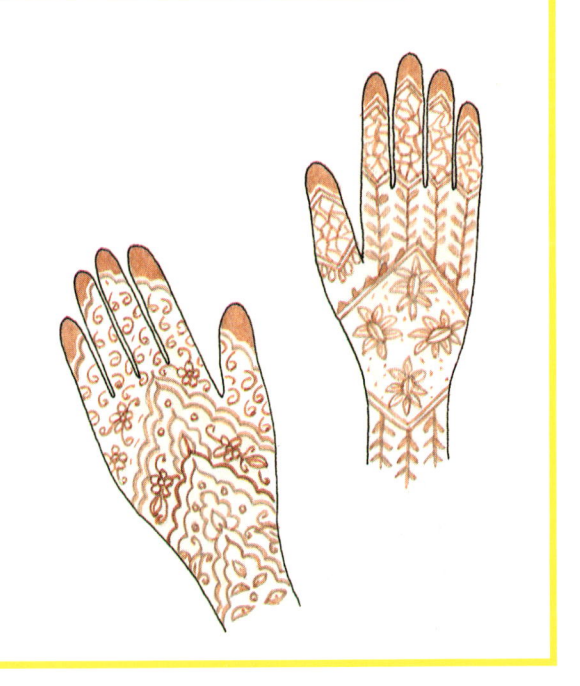

SARANGI

This one-stringed instrument comes from India. It can be plucked like a guitar, or played with a bow like a cello.

You will need:

cork
drill
fishing line (1m)
greaseproof paper
margarine tub
paste
pencil
piece of wood (3cm × 50cm × 1cm)
poster paints
scissors
tissue paper

Caution: woodworking tools can be dangerous. Ask an adult for help.

1 Trace round the top of an empty margarine tub on to a piece of greaseproof paper. Draw another circle about 2cm bigger round the outside.

2 Cut round the larger circle, then use as a template to cut three more greaseproof paper circles and four tissue paper circles.

3 Firmly stick one of the greaseproof circles over the top of the plastic tub, then paste on a tissue circle, pulling it gently to avoid wrinkles. Leave to dry.

4 Repeat 3 until you have used all the paper, making sure that each layer is pulled tightly across the tub and dry before adding the next.

5 Cut slits either side of the tub, big enough for the wood to fit through.

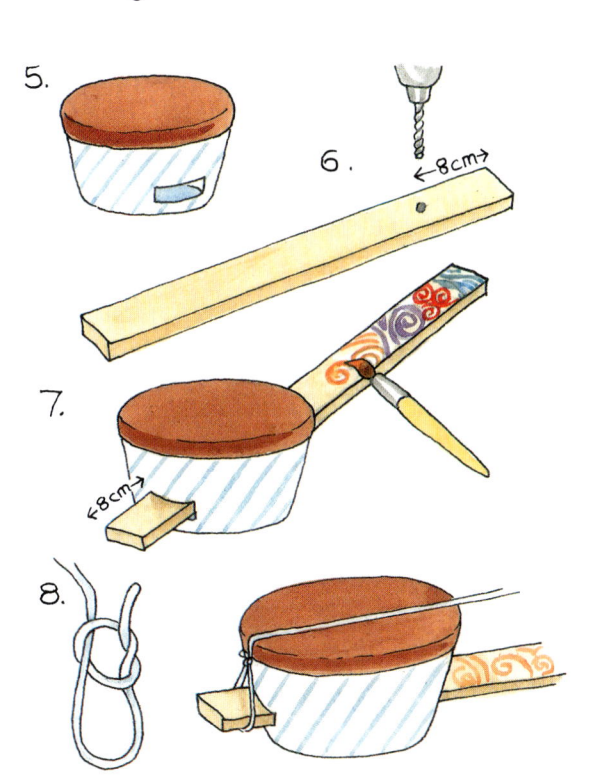

6 Bore a hole at a spot 8cm from one end of the piece of wood.

7 Push the other end through the tub until about 8cm juts out of the other side. Decorate with paints.

8 Tie a slip knot in the fishing line as shown. Hook the loop over the short end of the wood, then pull tightly over the tub and tie through the hole at the other end.

9 Cut the cork in half and stick under the string as a bridge.

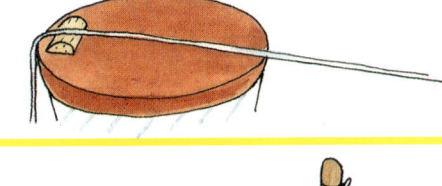

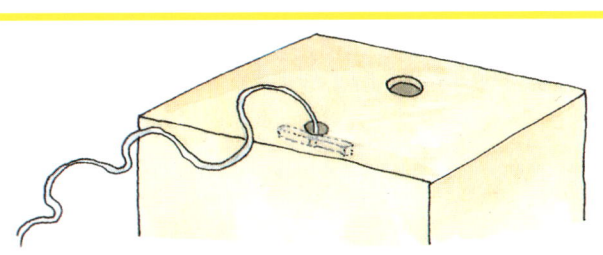

To make a double bass. Tie a small stick to the end of a piece of string, then thread the other end through the top of a cardboard box so that the stick is held inside. Make a larger hole in the top of the box and push a broom handle through it. Tie the string to the top of the broom handle, then pluck the string to make a sound.

JAPANESE DRUM

Carry this drum in a carnival procession or use it to accompany a dance or play. As you twist the handle, the beads flick excitedly against the sound box.

You will need:

2 beads
paints
paste
pencil
scissors
stick or garden cane
sticky tape
string
white paper
wooden cheese box

1 Place the box lid on a piece of white paper and draw round the edge.

2 Cut out the circle and stick to the lid, then decorate with a colourful picture or pattern.

3 Cut away a small section from the side of the box and insert the stick. Tape the stick to the base of the box as shown.

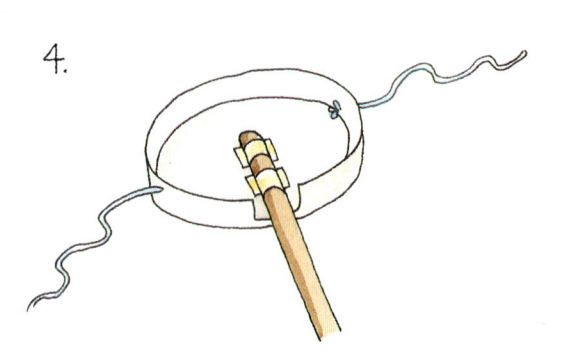

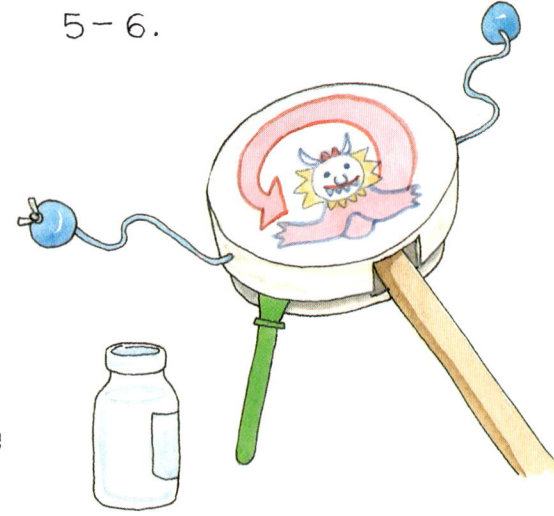

4 Pierce a hole in each side of the box. Knot two pieces of string and thread through each hole.

5 Stick the lid firmly over the base.

6 Tie a bead on to the end of each piece of string.

7 To play, twist the handle and allow the beads to flick against the box.

You can make a similar sound by cutting 1cm × 10cm strips from a plastic bottle and taping them to a saucepan, margarine tub or milk bottle. Flick to produce a clicking effect.

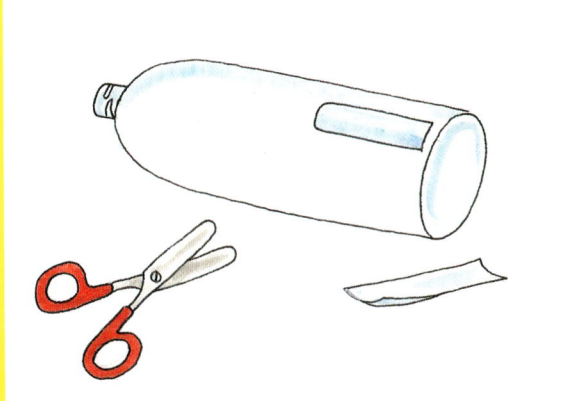

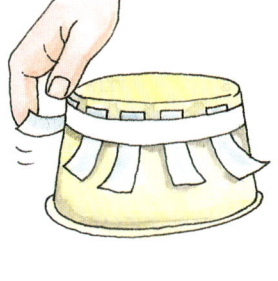

TWEETERS

Like the bull-roarer, an ancient instrument from New Guinea, tweeters are swung wildly above the head. Safest to play outside!

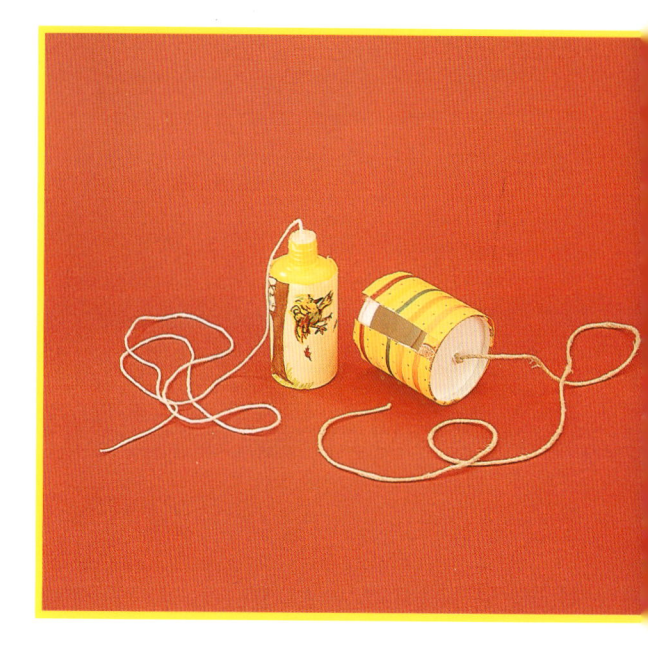

You will need:

matchstick
paste
patterned paper
plastic tub with lid
scissors
sticky tape
string

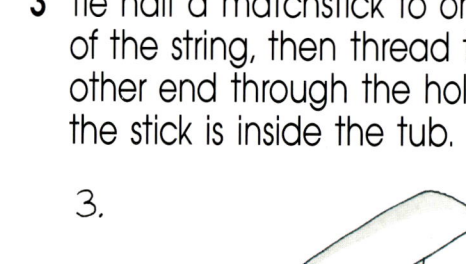

1 Cut a slit 1cm wide into the side of the plastic tub and make a small hole in the bottom.

2 Cut a length of string about 30cm long.

3 Tie half a matchstick to one end of the string, then thread the other end through the hole so the stick is inside the tub.

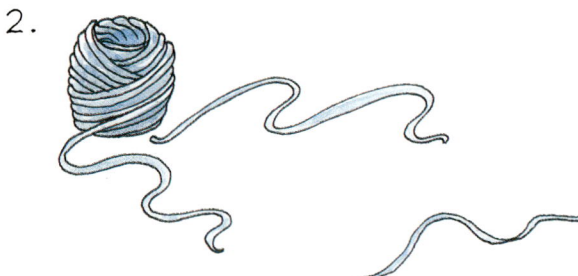

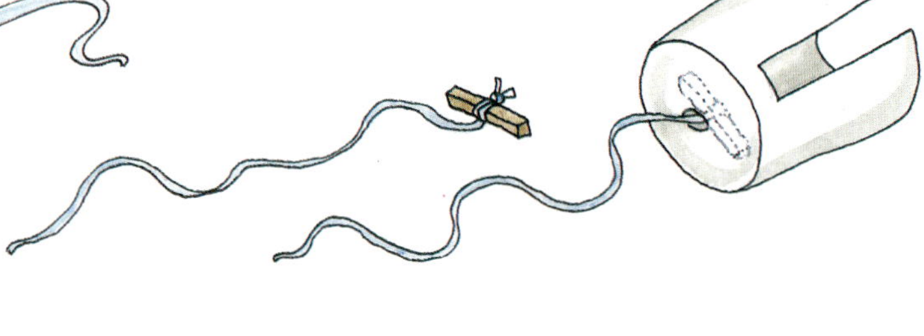

4 Tape the lid firmly in place.

5 Cover with brightly patterned paper, taking care to leave the slit open.

6 Swing the tub round on the end of the string and hear it 'tweeting'.

7 Experiment using different size bottles and cartons to make different sounds.

Another way to make a note is to blow gently across the top of a glass bottle. Pour some water into the bottle and you will hear a different note. Line up several bottles, each with a different amount of water, and you will have enough notes to play a tune.

SOAP-HOLDER

Keep your soap-holder to brighten up your own bathroom, or give it to a friend as a present.

You will need:

clay
damp cloth
knife
small margarine tub
paint
pencil
sponge
slip and brush
varnish
water

1 Cover the margarine tub with a damp cloth.

2 Roll out a circular slab of clay and lay it over the upturned tub.

3 Trim the extra clay from the base and squeeze the folds of clay together at either side. One side will become the tail, the other the neck.

4 Roll out another slab of clay and cut out two wings and a crest as shown.

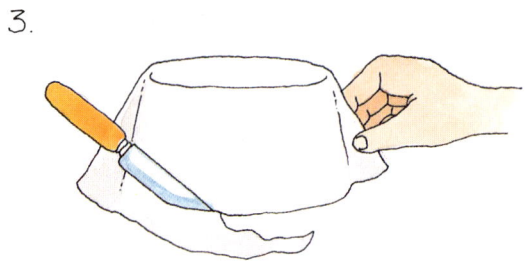

5 Roll a ball to make the head. Pull some clay forward and shape into a beak. Roll two small balls of clay for the eyes and stick them to the head with slip.

6 When the body is firm to the touch, remove it gently from the margarine tub and stick on the wings, head and crest as shown.

7 Smooth all the edges with a sponge.

8 Using the pencil, scratch feather patterns on the wings and tail.

9 Leave to harden, then paint and varnish.

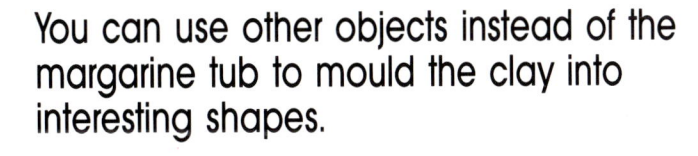

You can use other objects instead of the margarine tub to mould the clay into interesting shapes.

a plastic bottle top

a pebble

the lid from a screw-top jar

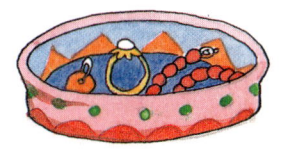

pot for small flowers or grasses

ladybird paperweight

trinket tray

59

SOLITAIRE

This game is easy to make and can be played alone or with a friend. Decorate the board and marbles in any style you like to make your own personal set.

You will need:

clay
marble
paint
rolling pin
sponge
varnish
water

1-2.

this thick

3-4.

1 Roll out a slab of clay, about 2cm thick.

2 Cut out a large circle – use a dinner plate or something similar to guide you.

3 Dent the clay with a marble. Follow the pattern shown.

4 Smooth the surface with a damp sponge.

5 Make a clay marble by rolling a small piece of clay in the palms of your hands. Do this another thirty-two times!

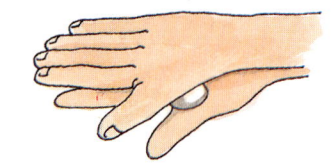

5.

60

6 Leave to harden, then paint and varnish. One marble should be a different colour from the rest.

To play solitaire

Place the marbles on the board, leaving the centre hole empty. A marble moves by jumping backwards, or forwards, or sideways over another marble into an empty hole. The marble that is jumped over is then taken away. The aim is to remove all the marbles from the board in this way, until only one remains.

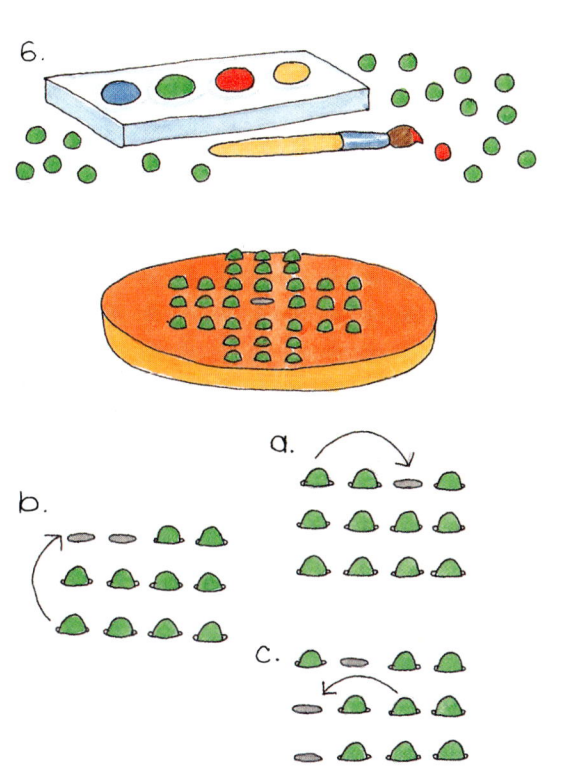

Fox and Geese (a game to play with a friend).

Lay out fourteen marbles as shown – one fox and thirteen geese.

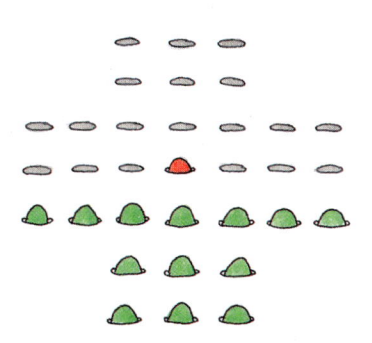

The geese can move one hole at a time in any direction. The fox can move only if he can jump over a goose and land in an empty hole. He then removes the goose from the board. The geese must try to hem the fox in so that he cannot move.

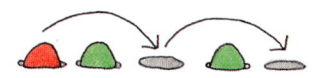

A fox may catch two geese at a time

DINOSAURS

Dinosaurs are easy to make and are cheaper to keep than pets!

You will need:

clay
nail
paint
slip and brush
varnish
water

1 Roll a sausage of clay, thicker in the middle than at the ends.

2 Shape one end to make a head as shown and pinch the other to make a pointed tail.

3 Roll four thick sausages for the legs and stick them to the body with slip.

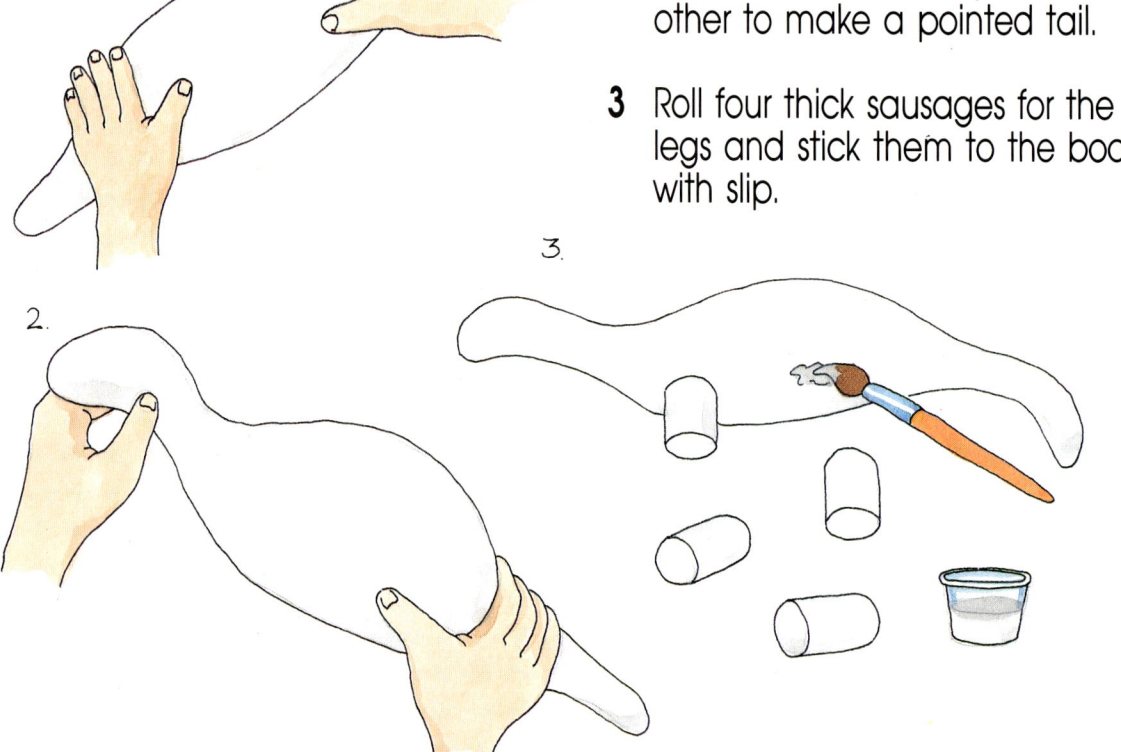

4.

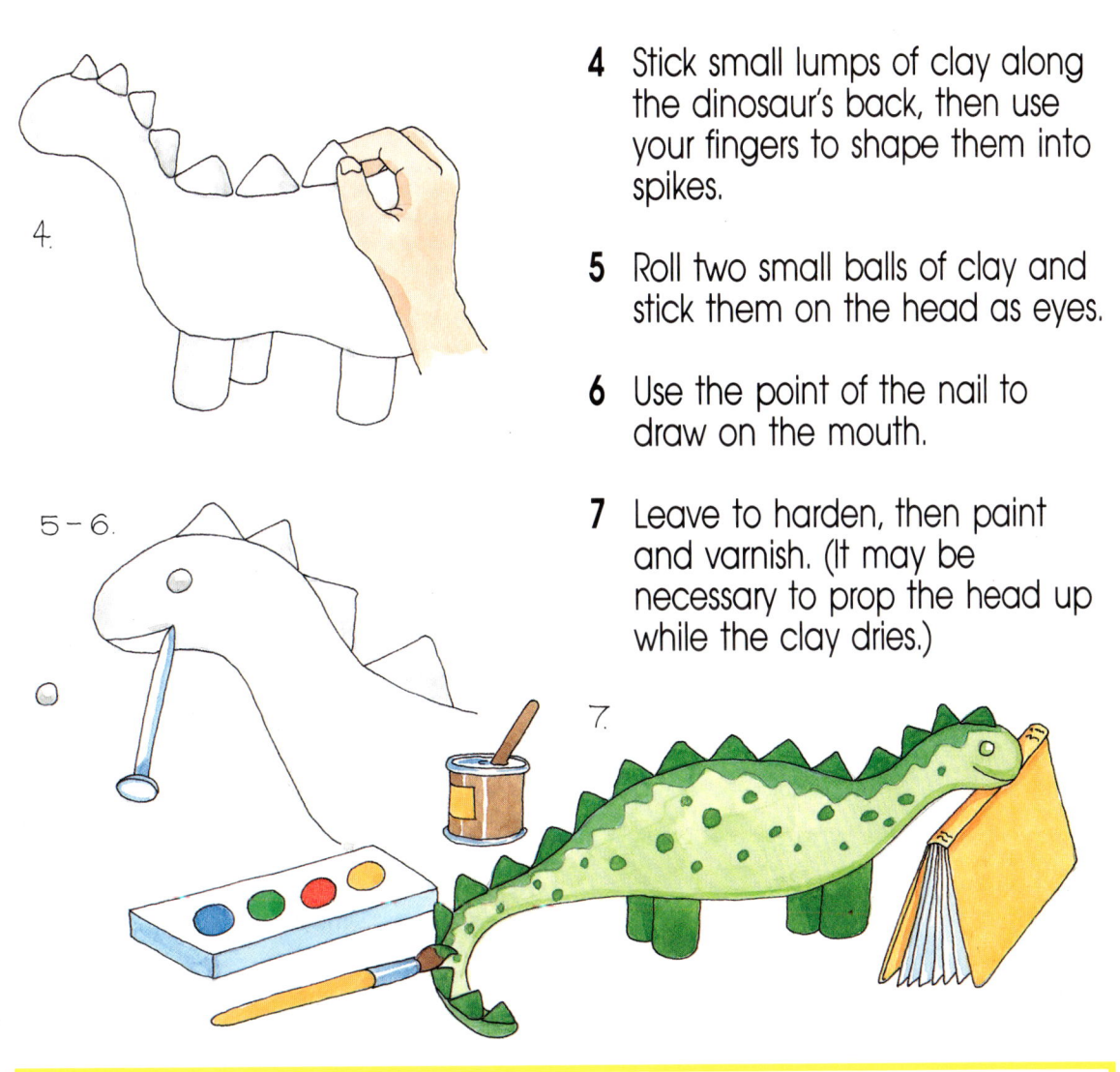

5–6.

4 Stick small lumps of clay along the dinosaur's back, then use your fingers to shape them into spikes.

5 Roll two small balls of clay and stick them on the head as eyes.

6 Use the point of the nail to draw on the mouth.

7 Leave to harden, then paint and varnish. (It may be necessary to prop the head up while the clay dries.)

7.

You can make many more animals in the same way. Here are some examples. I am sure you can think of your own.

INDEX

acrobat 32
acrobatic angler 36

bird nest potatoes 14
bottled herbs 10

Chinese dragon 34
Chinese dragon salad 18

dart and launcher 42
desk tidy 22
dinosaurs 62
diving octopus 38

Eastern delights 16

fabric painting 24
face painting 50
fish mobile 46

gift boxes 44
glass prints 48
greetings cards 20

helicopter 40

Japanese drum 54
jewellery 8

miniature garden 12
moving pictures 28

photograph tree 4

repeating patterns 6

sarangi 52
soap-holder 58
solitaire 60

tie and dye scarf 26
tweeters 56

window picture 30